Breaking the Tablets

Breaking the Tablets

Jewish Theology After the Shoah

David Weiss Halivni

Edited and Introduced by
Peter Ochs

ROWMAN & LITTLEFIELD PUBLISHERS, INC.
Lanham • Boulder • New York • Toronto • Plymouth, UK

ROWMAN & LITTLEFIELD PUBLISHERS, INC.

Published in the United States of America
by Rowman & Littlefield Publishers, Inc.
A wholly owned subsidiary of The Rowman & Littlefield Publishing Group,
Inc.
4501 Forbes Boulevard, Suite 200, Lanham, Maryland 20706
www.rowmanlittlefield.com

Estover Road
Plymouth PL6 7PY
United Kingdom

British Library Cataloguing in Publication Information Available

Library of Congress Cataloging-in-Publication Data

Halivni, David.
  Breaking the tablets : Jewish theology after the Shoah / David Weiss
Halivni ; edited and introduced by Peter Ochs.
    p. cm.
  Includes index.
  ISBN-13: 978-0-7425-5220-3 (cloth : alk. paper)
  ISBN-10: 0-7425-5220-9 (cloth : alk. paper)
  ISBN-13: 978-0-7425-5221-0 (pbk. : alk. paper)
  ISBN-10: 0-7425-5221-7 (pbk. : alk. paper)
  1. Holocaust (Jewish theology) 2. Holocaust, Jewish (1939-1945)—
Influence 3. God (Judaism) 4. Prayer—Judaism. 5. Rabbinical literature—
History and criticism. 6. Bible. O.T. Pentateuch—Criticism, interpretation,
etc. I. Ochs, Peter. II. Title.
  BM645.H6H35 2007
  296.3'1174—dc22   2007011991

Printed in the United States of America

♾™ The paper used in this publication meets the minimum requirements
of American National Standard for Information Sciences—Permanence of
Paper for Printed Library Materials, ANSI/NISO Z39.48-1992.

Dedicated to the row of five that arrived in Auschwitz on May 15, 1944, consisting of grandfather, mother, aunt, sister, and myself: grandfather and mother destined to the gas chambers, aunt and sister to prolonged suffering until they succumbed, and I survived alone to tell, to remind, and to demand. . . .

If only the first Tablets had not been broken, then Israel would not have forgotten the Torah.

('*Eruvin 54a*)

Contents

Note to Readers   ix

Prologue: Between Sinai and Auschwitz   x

Editor's Introduction   xii

1   Prayer in the Shoah   1

2   Restoring Scripture   43

3   Breaking the Tablets and Begetting the Oral Law   65

4   Epilogue: Between Auschwitz and Sinai   103

Contemporary Works Cited   117

Index of Biblical and Rabbinic Sources   121

General Index   129

About the Author   135

About the Editor   137

Note to Readers

As in David Halivni's previous books in English, Hebrew will be transliterated in this book following a popular orthography rather than linguists' conventions. The following alphabet will be adopted: -, b/v, g, d, h, v, z, ch, t, y, kh, l, m, n, s,-, p/f, k, r, s/sh, t; a, i, o, u.

Unless otherwise noted, Talmudic references will be to the Babylonian Talmud.

Prologue:
Between Sinai and Auschwitz

David Weiss Halivni

There were two major theological events in Jewish history, Revelation at Sinai and revelation at Auschwitz. The former was a revelation of God's Presence, the latter a revelation of God's absence; the former indicated God's nearness to us, the latter God's distance. At Sinai, God appeared before Israel, addressed us, and gave us instructions; at Auschwitz, God absented Himself from Israel, abandoned us, and handed us over to the enemy. In between these two periods, Israel's spiritual history took place, moving between God's embracing us at Sinai and God's withdrawing from us at Auschwitz, between divine intervention and divine abandonment, between our sense of connection and our sense of detachment. Every aspect of spiritual life is affected by this movement: the way we believe, the way we pray, the way we study His Torah, and the way we make ritual decisions. The way we view His connection to us affects our place and purpose in the universe. Our catechism and our beliefs are formed by it. Prayer is certainly affected by this movement, whether we concentrate on extolling God's greatness, lamenting His inaccessibility, or pleading that He should not discard us, that "He should not take away the Holy Spirit from us," that He should continue to abide among us.

But how does this movement affect the study of Torah and the halakhic and theological decisions that issue from this study? I have dedicated this book to answering this question. In chapter 1, "Prayer in the Shoah," I recollect how we prayed in the camps for God to return to us, to rule over humanity once again. I note, thereby, the difference between praying in God's presence and in His apparent absence. In chapter 2, "Restoring Scripture," I reflect on how our reception and study of Torah has changed through the epochs of God's increasing distance: from the days when the rabbinic sages themselves were touched, on occasion, by God's immediate presence, to the terrible days of God's absence during the Shoah. In chapter 3, "Breaking the Tablets and Begetting the Oral Law," I offer a scholarly review of the history of the Oral Law, examining how, in case after case, the later Amoraic and medieval notion of a separate oral law contradicts the evidence of Scripture and of the Tannaitic literatures. The implication is that, in God's absence, the words of even great sages are merely human words, prone to human error. In chapter 4, "Epilogue: Between Auschwitz and Sinai," I return to the theme of this prologue: how, having faced God's absence, we pray for Him to rule over us once again and, in His nearness, to illumine the meaning of His Torah. In the meantime, our study turns toward recovering the plain sense of Torah, behind the maculations of the human hand.

Editor's Introduction[*]

Peter Ochs

David Weiss Halivni is recognized as one of the postwar generation's greatest Talmudic scholars. He is Professor Emeritus of Classical Jewish Civilization at Columbia University and former head of the Talmud Department of the Jewish Theological Seminary. Known primarily for his multivolume work of Talmudic commentary, still in progress, Halivni is also author of more general works on the character and history of Talmudic literature. He is founder and rector of the Institute of Traditional Judaism (in Teaneck, New Jersey) and for many years the *mara d'atra* of a modern Orthodox synagogue in the Upper West Side of New York. Halivni was born in 1927 in a small village in the Ukraine, but from the age of four he was raised by his grandfather in Sighet, Romania. Halivni was a child prodigy in the Talmud who would at times be brought from town to town to display his remarkable knowledge of the entire corpus of the Talmud. In 1943, at the age of fifteen, he was ordained as a rabbi. That same year, however, Sighet was occupied by the Nazis. As narrated in his memoir, *The Book and the Sword*, Halivni was taken to the concentration camps Auschwitz and Bergen-Belsen and the labor camp Wolfsburg. The camps consumed his entire family.

---

[*] I dedicate my editorial work on this book and this introduction to my parents-in-law, Barbara and Bernard Grandis. I have discussed these topics with them for years, and their questions and reflections have helped inspire my work with Dr. Halivni. May they find theological consolation through his words.

This book is offered in answer to the questions many of us have asked Halivni, and not only out of historical interest but also because we also ask these questions of ourselves. We have, first of all, asked him questions that speak to our own religious lives after the Shoah. For example, "What does it mean for you to be religious after the Shoah? How do you still pray? And what, after those years of horror, has motivated you to invest your energies into this work of recovering and repairing the Talmud?"

There is a pressing reason why many of us believe it is important to ask these questions and to publish some of Halivni's answers in this volume. It is that we cannot imagine Judaism without some form of Jewish theology, and we cannot today put our trust in a Jewish theology that has not survived the Shoah. We cannot imagine what Jewish theology means other than what we can observe in lives of Torah: lives, that is, of flesh and blood human beings who have studied words of Torah and sought to embody them in their everyday lives. We cannot therefore imagine speaking of "Jewish theology surviving the Shoah" unless we can speak in some detail of people who have actually sought to embody Torah in their lives, have suffered life in the camps, and have appeared to have lived lives of Torah afterward. What we mean by "Jewish theology after the Shoah" is the character of those lives lived after the Shoah. One must encounter and study many such lives to be able to speak more generally of what Judaism looks like after the Shoah.[1] This is a volume about just one of those lives.

Many of us are drawn to study Halivni's life, in particular, not only because he has sought a life of Jewish piety but also because he has made the literature that is foundational to Jewish piety—the Mishnah and the Talmud—the subject of exhaustive, scientific study. That leads some of us to ask Halivni somewhat more scholarly questions about his life of Talmud study after the Shoah. For example, "What shall we learn from the fact that you were a passionate student of Talmud both before and after the Shoah? Did the Talmud provide a refuge for you through those years? And what shall we learn from the fact that, after the Shoah, you undertook a lifetime project of "repairing" the Talmud? Is this repair a matter of scholarship for its own sake, or is it a mark of some change in the meaning of Talmud and Torah before and after the Shoah? Shall we draw any general lesson from the title of your life's work, *Sources and Traditions* (*Mekorot Umasorot*)? Do you mean to suggest that the tradition has not survived the Shoah unscathed but that it must be renewed by being brought back to its 'sources'? Does Torah live on after this loss and death only through some renewal, and do you offer your work as part of such a renewal? Or do you literally mean what you say in *Midrash, Mishnah, and Gemara*: that you maintain a strict divide between Talmudic scholarship and religious practice, so that your Talmudic criticism does not have a broader, religious meaning?"

As a reader of Halivni's work over the past twenty-five years, I have the impression that his effort both divides and does not divide the spheres of academic scholarship and everyday religious life. I believe the reason is that, during the latter years of his academic career, the character of academic scholarship is itself changing because of the impact of the Shoah and of other profound crises in modern Western civilization. In the next section, I offer a brief history of these changes in scholarship and how Halivni's work speaks to them.

DIVISIONS AND INTEGRATIONS
IN RECENT TALMUDIC SCHOLARSHIP

In the decades before and immediately after the Shoah, Jewish academic scholarship drew fairly sharp lines between traditional learning (or *lernen*) and the "science of Judaism" (*das Wissenschaft des Judentums*, as it was promoted by the nineteenth-century progenitors of Jewish academic study, among them Leopold Zunz and Heinrich Graetz). As they entered the Western university, Jewish scholars sought to leave the methods of the yeshivah at home, along with confessions of traditional and personal piety, and dedicate their studies to the universal norms and methods of the academic study of history and literature. In Judah Leib Gordon's Enlightenment formulation, this meant being a Jew at home and a man on the street; in Samson Raphael Hirsch's neo-Orthodox rebuttal, it was "Torah im derekh erets," strict observance of Torah alongside an embrace of Western culture. In earlier writings, Halivni came close to Hirsch's logic when he sought to account for the divide between his halakhic observance and his critical science of Talmud:

> As we have continually stressed, our modern exegetical preference for *peshat* need not impinge upon the realm of practical halakha. A religious Jew may critically study the text of the Bible even with its occasionally disfigured *peshat*, yet his halakhic allegiance must be to rabbinic *derash*.[2]

Over the past two to three decades, however, university scholars have grown more cautious about the universality and, at times, even the reliability of their scientific methods of study. The horrors of both world wars raised questions, little by little, about some of the modern university's most cherished assumptions: that, for example, the university's best thinkers could discern universal standards for conducting scientific inquiry; that they could lay aside all personal, national, and religious commitments for the sake of uncovering scientific truths; and that, among these truths, they could discern universal standards for human conduct or, at least, standards for evaluating the good or bad consequences of the codes of ethics we have inherited. Losing faith in what now seem like the "old" Enlightenment hopes for human reason, some scholars have turned to a more thoroughgoing skepticism: as if each social group will have its own ethics with no rational way to adjudicate conflicts between one set of ethics and another and as if each school of thinkers will have its own standards of reason with no more general standard for judging among these. Some of the skeptics argue, in fact, that there is no ground for maintaining the "old" divisions between public standards of academic science and private beliefs (including religious beliefs): that what we call "universal reason" may in fact display the local interests of certain social and religious groups, while our religion- or gender- or politically based beliefs may in fact make significant contributions to the ways we reason, more deeply, about the world at large.

Recent Jewish scholarship reflects this general trend. Some scholars of Judaism defend the "older" modern dichotomy between science (as universal and objective inquiry) and religious belief (as strictly local and personal or subjective). Others join the skeptics: portraying Jewish scholarship, in this instance, as a way to retell and describe the events and literatures of the Jewish people without presuming to demonstrate the truth or falsity of any general theories about this people and its beliefs. Jewish scholars were, in fact, among influential proponents of this kind of skepticism, in several cases citing the literature of the Talmud as a major resource.[3] Some scholars of the rabbinic literature have since offered even stronger suggestions that—to speak metaphorically—the rabbinic sages do not sit passively while we modern scholars take their picture, that is, while we examine them with the tools of literary and historical science.[4] Instead, the sages insist on being part of the action, photographing us as much as we photograph them. There are some dimensions of rabbinic literature, in other words, that elude the concepts and methods of strictly modern scholarship. More than that, modern researchers who try to hear the rabbinic texts in the texts' own terms find that the way they hear is affected by what they hear. In Fraade's terms, there is a "shuttling back and forth" between what the texts say and how they are received, a dialogical relation between the texts' formation and their reception.[5]

Some of these skeptics have thus come to look to the Talmudic literature not only as a subject for academic study but also as a source of concepts and methods for use in the academic study of rabbinic literature—or even of other literatures not only within Jewish tradition but also within other traditions and civilizations. In this way, skepticism about the reach of modern Western methods of inquiry has given rise, unexpectedly, to what we may label a *third direction of academic study*. This third direction neither reaffirms the rational standards of the modern academy nor raises doubts about all rational standards. Instead, it employs the tools of modern inquiry in a humble way as a means of approaching new literatures and subjects of study, learning new patterns of reasoning from them, and then engaging them in what these scholars hope will be a mutually fruitful dialogue. In this case, it is dialogue between Talmudic literature and the tools of modern literary and historical science.

Halivni's corpus of writings contributes to all three of these contemporary forms of Jewish scholarship but displays its overall coherence only when read according to the third. When read this way, furthermore, his Talmudic science and his religious piety need no longer be interpreted as mutually exclusive. I believe that, until recently, Halivni described his own work in those either/or terms because, with the great majority of his peers and readers, he assumed that Jewish scholarship imposed those terms: that, in its classic form, modern scholarship was insulated from any issues of religious practice, while more recent, postmodern scholarship insulated itself from any truth claims—academic or religious. More recently, however, Halivni has begun to write about his Talmudic scholarship within the terms of this third approach. This means he has begun to redescribe his religious practice and Talmudic science as distinct yet complementary, rather than mutually exclusive, elements of his overall endeavor. I recall how painful it was for him to write—and lecture about—his Holocaust memoir, *The Book and the Sword*. However painful it has been for him to return to such themes in *Breaking the Tablets*, the effort also appears to bring coherence to the way he describes his work. Overall, Halivni's more general writings discuss the methods of interpretation, the sense of history, and the theological commitments that underlie his Talmudic commentaries and reconstructions in *Mekorot Umasorot*. In *Midrash, Mishnah, and Gemara*, in *Peshat and Derash*, and to some degree in *Revelation Restored*, he attends to issues of Talmudic scholarship, above all, and engages in conversation with rabbinic scholars throughout the ages, with the *Tannaim* first and foremost and, secondarily, with contemporary scientists of the Talmud. These conversations address two issues in particular. One is the gradual (and, in his eyes, unfortunate) evolution of rabbinic commentary away from active dialogue with the plain sense of sacred texts and toward dogmatic and defensive pronouncements on behalf of some given tradition of religious practice. The second issue is how to respect the independence of both scientific scholarship of the Talmud and halakhic practice so that neither endeavor imposes itself on the other.

Since (and partly in) *Revelation Restored*, however, Halivni's general writings have gradually reframed each of these issues, and *Breaking the Tablets* not only applies the new frames but also begins to identify and account for them. On the one hand, Halivni attributes the evolution of rabbinic interpretation to the consequences of God's moving away from Israel and not only to the consequences of "Israel's sins," *chate'u yisrael*. From this perspective, rabbinic scholarship is conditioned by a divine and cosmic drama that the congregation of Israel (and humankind around it) can influence only modestly and only over the long run of history. On the other hand, Halivni attends less to the boundaries between science and piety and more to the boundaries between humanity and God. The central drama is no longer how to promote scientific study while protecting halakhic tradition. It is how, in God's near-absence, scientists of Bible and Talmud must accept responsibility for searching out the plain sense of God's word while they pray, urgently, for Him to come near again. Outright idolatry, Halivni now suggests, is an act of defiance that takes place only in God's presence or near presence. In this time of God's great distance, we are not in danger of serving other gods but of failing to recognize that we no longer know clearly how to serve this One. The sin, we might say, is acting as if we were not as surrounded by failures, errors, blemishes, and disappointments as we are. The sin is seeking certainty too quickly and on inadequate grounds: trusting our intuitions, habits, memories, and religious authorities more than the evidence warrants. The sin is failing to see how dark this time is and how distant God remains.

But is this not to abandon hope and faith? No. As I read Halivni, this is not to abandon hope but, rather, to let go of the need for false hopes. It is to have faith in the God of truth, who may be distant but who has previously ruled over us and over humanity with great force; and it is to have hope that *He may do so again*. It is to have faith in the word and instruction God has already given us, much of whose plain sense is sufficiently clear to us that we can often distinguish right from wrong, good from bad, true from false. And it is to have hope that the instruments of reason God has given us will enable us clarify much of what remains unclear. It is to have faith in the redemptive acts God has performed in the past. Despite our knowledge that there are times—recent ones—when He has not come to us as redeemer, it is, nonetheless, to have hope that *He will once again hear our prayers and renew our days as of old*.

In this way, *Breaking the Tablets* contributes to the "third" approach to rabbinic scholarship mentioned previously, nurturing a dialogue between traditional and academic approaches to Talmudic literatures and practices. While Halivni has nurtured such a dialogue throughout his scholarly career, his current reflections on theology after the Shoah integrate science and faith in a distinctive way. The evolution in his thinking may reflect his having laid bare the utter loss that drives and shapes his life's work on the Talmud: the *pagam* (blemish, "maculation") and *pagua* (injury, abuse) that he observes in all dimensions of creation and even in what can be observed of the divine life. I believe his scholarship and faith are united by this traumatic observation. When he turns aside from this trauma—in a fashion also "covering over" its ubiquity—he may assimilate his reflections, to some degree, to the prevailing divisions between faith and science. But when, as in this volume, he does not turn aside, those divisions are overshadowed by the vastly more terrifying rift he sees dividing the promise of Sinai from the fact of Auschwitz.

To say the visions are "overshadowed" is not merely to offer a portrait of this survivor's inner emotions. For Halivni, the overshadowing may be a perception as real as any perception that informs his textual science or his study of history. Within the cloud of this overshadowing he may *see* science and halakhic practice as parts of different spheres of human endeavor that also share in a common destiny: sharing in a world of broken tablets and thus sharing in the same blemish (*pagam*) that mars everything that "God spoke and it was." As he sees them, science and the *halakhah* are therefore each in need of the same repair (*tikkun*); neither can be fully justified, warranted, and certain until something else occurs. For Halivni, this something is God's renewed presence among the people Israel and within the human realm: we cannot, apart from that presence, articulate what it would mean for us, but our prayers give voice to what we suffer in His absence and carry with them the hope that He would, at least, remove from us what He knows to be the ground of that suffering. Halivni's primary prayer during and after Auschwitz is that God would rule over us again as He did at Sinai. I understand this to include a prayer for God's drawing near enough, again, to reduce humanity's excessive freedoms and thus reduce its capacity for unlimited violence, in particular and in face of the God of Israel's seeming absence, violence against the people Israel. As I read Halivni, this is consequently a prayer for the people Israel's losing enough fear and insecurity that, when God drew near enough, Israel's sages could, without defensiveness or fear, follow his Instructions once again to repair the Torah and all the traditions of Torah learning so that the plain sense of the Law could be made clear. This is, in other words, the prayer that guides *Mekorot Umasorot*—"Sources and Traditions"—as a work of both scientific scholarship and religious piety. It is, in God's almost-absence, to adopt Talmudic science as a means of identifying blemishes on all levels of the Oral Law (of the traditions, *masorot*) while waiting, in the light of God's presence, to see the Word (the sources, *mekorot*) that remains when these blemishes are removed.

OVER THE BORDERS BETWEEN SCIENCE AND PIETY

Halivni appears to position his work on the way between Auschwitz and Sinai and very close to the former. By the measure of what lies behind and stands ahead, the corporate self-concerns of strict scientists on his one side and strict traditionalists on the other appear out of place, out of touch, out of this particular time in history and what it demands. Science is for him a tool of great promise and usefulness. But excessive worry about the borders of the academy, let alone single disciplines within it, appears like an effort to cover over the reality of what has happened in his lifetime, to cover up truth rather than pursue it. All the phenomena and behaviors and experiences and perceptions—beliefs, practices, visions, sufferings, and yearnings—that accompany Jewish social, personal, communal, religious, and spiritual life are sources of irreducible and irreplaceable evidence about the subject matter of the Talmud and the reception history of those who read, analyze, examine, and perform it. The halakhah belongs to this performance, but so does science.

For Halivni, religious piety is no threat to scientific objectivity since it is a source of his commitment to science as well as to the other aspects of halakhah. Religious piety is the tissue and texture of the literature he studies, and performance is a dimension of study. But excessive worry about the borders of one's tradition of piety also covers over what is really at stake at this time of threat and obligation. It is understandable that Jews would feel physically and spiritually insecure after the Shoah and that this insecurity would breed excessive efforts at individual and communal self-protection and defensiveness. But this is, nonetheless, precisely the wrong time, out of insecurity, to over-defend one's particular community—school, yeshivah, or denomination—of Jewish practice. Over-defense means covering over any signs of imperfection or error in one's traditions or literatures or practices. But, in this proximity to Auschwitz, there is no escaping signs of *pagam*—of physical and spiritual blemish—in every aspect of the creation, let alone in one's own tradition of learning and practice.

Breaking the Tablets is thus offered to both academic and religious readers as an approach to Talmudic scholarship that honors both science and tradition while also participating in a third kind of study that cannot be bound within either of their borders. The four chapters of *Breaking the Tablets* illustrate four dimensions of this study. In the next section, I briefly introduce the themes of these chapters as a way of introducing, as well, Halivni's contributions to each of these dimensions of work.

FOUR CHAPTERS AND FOUR DIMENSIONS OF STUDY

Chapter One: "Prayer in the Shoah"

This is a memoir of how Halivni prayed, in the concentration camps, for God to rule over us again. The memoir serves as a testimony to the fact of human history and of religious history that conditions the course of Halivni's study of the Talmud. It thereby serves as testimony, as well, to the historical and theological ground of Halivni's "third way" of approaching Talmudic scholarship: situating science, explicitly, within the existential and theological as well as communal and disciplinary presuppositions of the scientist.

Chapter Two: "Restoring Scripture"

This most recent of Halivni's writings uncovers the implications of his prayer in the Shoah for reorienting a history of Israel's reception of

Torah. God, he surmises, has grown increasingly distant from us since the time of the Tannaim, and we, as a result, have been left increasingly with words authored by ourselves alone. Halivni's response is, as a means of turning back toward Sinai, a practice of science and of prayer: plain-sense study of the marks of human effort and error in the Oral Law and prayer for the return of God's more intimate word. In the process, this chapter illustrates Halivni's *depth* (or *religious*) *historiography*: a way to glean, from tradition- and community-specific beliefs, practices, and experiences, academically useful hypotheses about dimensions of Israel's history of Torah study that are not otherwise visible to the scientist of text and history.

Chapter Three: "Breaking the Tablets and Begetting the Oral Law"

This lengthy chapter illustrates Halivni's central work of Talmudic criticism and how, as seen more clearly through the setting of this book, it contributes to his overall theological commitment. The topic is Halivni's plain-sense criticism of a rabbinic tendency, from the amoraic period to today, to misrepresent humanly authored Oral Law as divinely revealed Torah. A central lesson for this book's readers is that God's near-absence from this epoch of human history obligates us to examine, all the more assiduously, the effects of human freedom not only in recent social history but also in the long history of Israel's transmitting the Oral and Written Torah. Halivni's plain-sense science displays an aspect of what scholars call "negative theology": that is, of seeking to cut away what we know to be the effects of human error and of simple human finitude in the hope that what remains may obscure God's light this much less.

Chapter Four: "Epilogue: Between Auschwitz and Sinai"

Composed as a reflection on the work of this book as a whole, this chapter returns to the themes of the book's prologue and its first chapter. The liturgical message is that during the Shoah, we prayed that God might rule over us again, reduce His distance from us, and thereby reduce humanity's capacity to practice its freedom in evil ways. Now we pray the same prayer again so that by reducing His distance from us, He might enable us to see more clearly what He spoke to Moses and, thus, what our way of Torah should be. The book has thus moved from historical and theological witness, to "depth" historiography, to plain-sense scholarship, then again to depth historiography, and to prayer. Plain-sense scholarship occupies the most pages—life in this historical time weighs on us the heaviest and obligates us to devote greater time to science—but all four dimensions of study and practice share equally in the qualitative texture and normative light of this "third way" of rabbinic scholarship.

APPENDIX

Four Dimensions of Halivni's Talmudic Scholarship

For readers less familiar with Halivni's corpus of writings, here is a more detailed introduction to the four dimensions of scholarship that are displayed in his work.

Plain-Sense Science

Among the *rishonim*, or early medieval commentators, Halivni's heroes are the *pashtanim*, or those whose goal is to uncover the "plain sense" of the Bible, the Mishnah, and the Gemara. The greatest of these is the Rashbam (Rabbi Shmuel son of Meir, d. ca. 1158), whom Halivni calls, "The greatest exegete of the Middle Ages, who explored the apparent suggestions of the text even when these ran against the *halakhah*."[6] Noting the Rashbam's strict piety—"It is told that the Rashbam, walking with his eyes downcast (probably to avoid gazing at women), almost mounted a wagon drawn [against biblical law] by an ox and a donkey in tandem"—Halivni sees in him a predecessor who also separates the realms of science and strict observance. There is a difference between them, however:

> The Rashbam's peshat-oriented approach applied only to scriptures. In his study of the rabbinic sources, the Rashbam followed the Talmud even when its interpretations diverged from the *peshat* of the Mishnah. Study of the scriptures . . . was not a means to creating new laws in the Middle Ages. Study of Talmud, however, was. Therefore, whereas the Rashbam allowed his interpretations of scriptures to follow *peshat*, wherever it led, he could not allow himself the same luxury when studying the Talmud, the fount of definitive law.[7]

Halivni drew the discipline of plain study into Talmudic criticism as well.

According to Halivni, the dominant meaning of *peshat* among the Tannaim is the meaning of a text within its immediate literary context: how it coheres within the explicit narrative or argument or literary form of the section, chapter, and book in which it is found. One may say that to read the plain sense in this way is, simply, to read with common sense, to read a text as it asks it to be read in the manner of its own art or literature. This is not easy to do, however, since readers may not share the literary conventions and assumptions that accompany the text, since the texts may display the work of many levels of redaction and collection, and since we may bring to the text many habits and traditions of interpretation that regulate what we think we see in it. One may characterize Halivni's Talmudic science overall as a series of strategies to deconstruct or cut away multiple layers of these habits and traditions of reading and redacting (*masorot*) so as to "lay bare" each text's elemental "sources" (*mekorot*).

Levels of Plain Sense

In various sorts of biblical and rabbinic studies, one often comes across the term "literal meaning." When this term is not used in the sense of "plain sense" (as defined below), it may refer to any one of the following senses: (a) *The "true" intended sense.* The term may refer to a scholar's sense of "what the original text was intended to mean," that is, according to the intention of the divine author or of some human authors. This is a confused use of the term and does not appear, in this form, in Halivni's work. The biblical text scholar and theologian Hans Frei called this a kind of "ostensive reference"—that is, a way of claiming what the text referred to, outside itself, rather than how the text worked within itself.[8] Adapting his term, we may call this the "conceptually ostensive sense" since it refers to ideal meanings; (b) *The actual things in the world (events, persons, objects) to which the text referred.* This may refer to a scholar's sense of "what the original text was talking about in the world, or what events in the world gave rise to the text." This is another form of ostensive reference, this time to what lay outside the text in the everyday world; we might call it the "materially ostensive sense." For Halivni, this should be called the historical context of the text, not its meaning. Framed this way, contextual study is a significant part of Halivni's work; (c) *How the words of the text would likely have been received by its earliest communities of readers or listeners.*[9] This is one of the dominant senses of "literal meaning" for modern and more recent text historians. To uncover such meanings, text historians sift through many types and levels of evidence, form hypotheses about the most likely meanings of the text, and then test these hypotheses against the broadest judgments of the scholarly community. These hypotheses are complicated by the scholars' sense that they are dealing with many-layered texts, different parts of which may have been stitched together at different times, each of which would have spoken differently to different communities, including the "final" community of the final redactor. This is a major focus in Halivni's work in *Mekorot Umasorot*, a dimension I will label *plain-sense historiography*.

As a study of plain sense, Talmudic science shares certain general features of most kinds of science: for example, dedication to the truth no matter what and to the truth at all levels of what can be known, desire to make changes (in thinking or practice) on the basis of what truth appears to be, attention to observable evidence and to empirical proof as much as they can be found, the capacity to analyze or see the many parts of what we observe, the capacity to synthesize or perceive how the things we observe may contribute to greater patterns, active use of the imagination to generate ever-renewed accounts of what one has observed and ever-refined models of how to frame such accounts, willingness to change one's theories on the basis of counterevidence, and willingness to engage actively in dialogue with fellow scientists and to learn even from those who work with different assumptions and different models of inquiry.

There are certain features of any science, however, that are shaped by features that may be unique to its specific subject. The more specific the subgenre of study, the more difficult it is for the broader community of scholars to achieve general agreement on the identity and meaning of various features of the subject matter. In the case of Talmudic science, these are features unique on one level to literary studies, on another level to literary-legal studies, on another level to scriptural interpretation, and so on. I will apply the term *"deeper plain-sense historiography"* to genre-specific dimensions of Talmudic science. A considerable portion of *Mekorot Umasorot* belongs to this dimension of inquiry.

Major examples include Halivni's study of the phenomenon of "forced interpretation" (*dochok*), his study of the trope *halakhah le moshe misinai*, and his attention to a broad range of other tropes, metaphors, and methods of interpretation that are specific to the rabbinic literature. Other examples are typical of literary studies more broadly, such as Halivni's attention to the Talmud's tolerance for unresolved disagreement and for ambiguity and to the Talmud's assumption that many terms and claims lose their ambiguity only when they are put to practical use in specific contexts of life, law, or study. These contexts are not usually supplied by the texts themselves, which means that, to understand more ambiguous terms in the Talmud, scholars must be able to imagine various contexts in which they could be used. Many such contexts can be imagined only by those who have lived lives of Talmudic study and practice, which means that some dimensions of *deeper plain-sense historiography* are more apparent to practitioners (or at least former practitioners!), and this means that this region of Talmudic science is not well served by drawing too rigid a borderline between theory and practice, in this case Talmudic science and rabbinic life.

Science beyond the Plain Sense

At times, Halivni draws on his personal practices of text study, halakhah, and prayer for sources of insight into dimensions of the Talmud that cannot be assigned even to the "deeper plain sense" but that, he argues, still merit attention from academicians. To make scientific sense of his claim, I find it helpful to draw the following two distinctions. Within Talmudic science, we might distinguish between deeper plain-sense historiography and a third dimension of study we might label *"depth historiography"* (his own term is "transcendent history"; others suggest "religious historiography"[10]). We might define the latter as *a method of gleaning from tradition-specific beliefs and practices hypotheses about the history of Torah study that can be communicated to and tested by a more general scholarly community.* We might then draw a distinction between the academic use of tradition-specific knowledge, as exemplified by *depth historiography*, and its extra-academic use, which we might label *theological studies* or, in particular, *rabbinic theology*.

In earlier writings, Halivni acknowledged that his claims, for example, about *chate'u yisrael* ("the Sins of Israel") or Ezra's editorial work did not belong to customary historical science. He therefore labeled such claims "transcendent history" and suggested that they belonged to the "theological" part of his work rather than the scientific part *per se*. I do not sense that this was a natural divide in his work, however, since such claims played a significant part in linking different regions of his plain-sense studies together (for example, his work on Bible, Mishnah, Talmud, and halakhah). Halivni's current writing opens itself to a three-part distinction that makes more sense of the way he has actually practiced his science through the decades: plain-sense academic work, depth-historiographic work that draws academically useful hypotheses out of tradition-specific practices, and tradition-specific theology for use outside the academy. From this perspective, depth historiography is a unique mark of the "third approach" to Talmudic studies since it speaks both to the academy (as a source of speculative but useful hypotheses) and to specific communities of practice (as a resource for religious narrative, theodicy, and liturgical theology).

Halivni argues that, after the Shoah, Talmudic scholars have a responsibility to contribute their intuitions to the realm of depth history while clearly distinguishing this from the other two levels of inquiry.[11] His reasoning goes something like this. Say a scholar wants to know how to interpret the account, in Nehemiah 8:1–8, of Ezra's reading aloud from a scroll of Torah while Levites "helped the people to understand the Law." Plain-sense historians lack sufficient text and historical evidence to offer clear judgments about how close this "helping the people" came to the early rabbinic practice of plain sense or of midrashic interpretation. If this question lacked great significance for how Jews make sense of the Torah today, then Halivni might agree that there is no need for scholars to offer speculations beyond what they can clearly defend in the court of academic opinion. He believes this is an urgent question, however, because Ezra's "saving the Torah out of the fires of Exile" may be the closest prototype we have of how Jews may or may not save the Torah, today, from out of the fires of Auschwitz. Since religious Jews will strain, in any event, to construct their own responses, Halivni asks if it is not more prudent for scholars to strain for answers instead: that is, for those who are most disciplined by the study of text and history to share their best intuitions with us, with all the appropriate disclaimers about the genre of their claims (that they speak, speculatively, to depth history and not to the plain sense) but also without unnecessary worry about what fits or does not fit into current conventions of the academy. Halivni notes that the Talmud has, in fact, framed a detailed answer to this question. Although this answer does not speak to the needs of plain-sense history, it has several strengths: it does not contradict the narrative account or what we know of history; even if not demonstrable, it belongs to the realm of reasonable possibility; it coheres with the broader practice of Torah in the rabbinic community of its time; and it appears to serve the good: that is to say, one may argue that Jewish life is made better rather than worse by belief in this answer. On this basis, Halivni argues that scholars, rather than the general populace (*amkha*), are best qualified to match the effort of the Talmud today and draw plausible inferences from the Nehemiah narrative that may help guide Jewish religious life after the Shoah. Drawing this inference, moreover, is not mere mythopoesis; it is a poesis that gives publicly useful narrative form to inferences that are of specific use, in different ways, to the academy and to the religious communities.

Breaking the Tablets narrates several of Halivni's depth historical inferences, for example, about the "Sins of Israel" (*chate'u yisrael*), about Ezra, and about God's movement away from Israel between Sinai and Auschwitz. In the context of his "third approach" to rabbinic studies, these represent Halivni's narrative way of introducing theological doctrines (appropriate to communities of practitioners) and elemental rules of textual interpretation (appropriate to the academy and to tradition). The doctrines represent Halivni's conclusions about how some foundations of Jewish religious belief and practice are altered after the Shoah—and, thus, about how religious Jews may need to revise their understanding of Israel's relation to God and of Israel's practice of Torah. One purpose of *Breaking the Tablets* is to deliver these doctrines, at times explicitly (as in Halivni's pronouncement about how to pray after Shoah and about God's distance from us) and at times between the lines. Another purpose of the book is to deliver Halivni's elemental rules of textual interpretation: his conclusions about how scholars and practitioners alike need to study the texts of Torah to both serve and test these revised foundations of belief. These rules also appear both explicitly in the book—in claims, for example, about the sins of forced interpretation—and between the lines.

In the editor's introduction to "Restoring Scripture," I analyze Halivni's depth historiography on yet another level: as his means of laying bare and revising the elemental presuppositions of his practice of Talmudic study. From this perspective, depth historiography revisits and revises the assumptions of both science and pious practice at a time of radical change in Judaism. Depth historiography tends to appear in narrative form as a form of indirect description, since there is no direct way to describe the assumptions that underlie one's very act of description, let alone an attempt to revise those assumptions. It is thus Halivni's means of saying that the Shoah has brought the elemental assumptions of twentieth-century religious Judaism into question. To engage in *tikkun talmud* and *tikkun torah*—the repair of Talmud and the repair of Torah—is to revise these assumptions and thereby contribute to the restoration of religious Judaism after Shoah.

NOTES

I am grateful to two University of Virginia graduate students, Daniel Weiss and Brantley Craig, who offered critical editorial assistance and advice in the preparation of this book.

1. Halivni concludes chapter 1, "Prayer in the Shoah," with a selected bibliography of theological responses to the Shoah, especially among orthodox survivors. See also the recent writings of Gershon Greenberg, one of whose on-going projects is to review "Ultra-Orthodox Reflections on the Holocaust, 1945 to the Present" (also the title of a recent essay of his, © 2002 in ms.). This essay is the most significant survey I have seen of the theologies of ultra-Orthodox survivors, along with Greenberg's essay Holocaust and Musar for the Telsiai Yeshivah," Avraham Yitshak and Eliyahu Meir Bloch (2002 in ms.). See also his essays "Between Holocaust and Redemption: Silence, Cognition, and Eclipse" and "Ultra-Orthodox Jewish Thought about the Holocaust since World War II," in *The Impact of the Holocaust on Jewish Theology*, ed. Steven T. Katz (New York: New York University Press, 2005): 110–31, 132–60. Endnotes to the latter essays also include an extensive bibliography on additional sources as well as on several other key essays of his. In "Ultra-Orthodox Reflections," Greenberg cites the following significant primary sources:

> The historical dimension of the postwar Ultra-orthodox response relation has been researched by Dan Michman, "Hashpa'ah Hashoah al Hayadut Hadatit," in Tenuot Yesod Be'am Hayehudi Be'ikvot Hashoah, ed. Yisrael Gutman (Jerusalem: 1995–1996): 176–77; Kimmy Kaplan, "Have Many Lies Accumulated in History Books? The Holocaust in Ashkenazi Haredi Historical Consciousness in Israel," *Yad Vashem Studies* 29 (2001): 321–78; and "Hahevrah Hahareidit Be'yisrael Ve'yahasah Lashoah-Keriyah Hadashah," *Alpayim* 17 (1999): 176–77; and Amos Goldberg, "Hashoah Be'itonut Hahareidit Bein Zikaron Lehadhakah," *Yahadut Zemanenu* 11–12 (1997/98): 155–206 (p. 35n1).

2. David Weiss Halivni, *Peshat and Derash: Plain and Applied Meaning in Rabbinic Exegesis* (Oxford: Oxford University Press, 1991), 154.

3. Among Jewish philosophers, for example, Franz Rosenzweig (German Jew, d. 1929) argued, out of the sources of Judaism, that human reasoning

is not an activity of seeing clear facts and deducing clear inferences but of "speech thinking" (*Sprachdenken*): articulating to someone on some given occasion how certain phenomena would (given certain presuppositions) call us to act. Emmanuel Levinas (French Jew, d. 1995) argued that conventional human reasoning tends to cut us off, in fact, from the evidences and demands of any other voice than our own: to know is to have one's otherwise solipsistic ways of knowing interrupted by the voice of the other and the Other. Levinas draws his account of this voice from Talmudic sources and attributes his deepest insights on this matter to his Talmud teacher R. Chouchani. The literary scholar Susan Handelman was one of the first to number Rosenzweig, Levinas, and their Jewish philosophic peers among the progenitors of what academics call the "postmodern movement" (and I am calling "skepticism") and to argue that this postmodernism comes from a rabbinic practice of midrashic text interpretation. See, for example, S. Handelman, *The Slayers of Moses* (Albany: State University of New York Press, 1982).

4. Among such authors (with illustrative writings) are Max Kadushin, *The Rabbinic Mind* (New York: Bloch, 1972 [orig. 1952]); Jose Faur, *Golden Doves with Silver Dots* (Tampa: University of South Florida, 2000 [orig. 1984]); Daniel Boyarin, *Intertextuality and the Reading of* Midrash (Bloomington: Indiana University Press, 1990); Steven Fraade (see note 5); and Tamar Ross, *Expanding the Palace of Torah: Orthodoxy and Feminism* (Boston: Brandeis University Press, 2004).

5. Steven Fraade, *From Tradition to Commentary: Torah and Its Interpretation in the Midrash Sifre to Deuteronomy* (Albany: State University of New York Press, 1991), 21, passim.

6. David Weiss Halivni, *Revelation Restored: Divine Writ and Critical Responses* (Boulder, CO: Westview Press, 1997): 80.

7. Halivni, *Revelation Restored*, 80.

8. See Hans Frei, *The Eclipse of Biblical Narrative: A Study in Eighteenth and Nineteenth Century Hermeneutics* (New Haven, CT: Yale University Press, 1980), passim.

9. The biblical scholar Moshe Greenberg calls this the text's "ideal reader." See M. Greenberg, "The Vision of Jerusalem in Ezekiel 8–11: A Holistic Interpretation," in *The Divine Helmsman, Studies on God's Control of Human Events, Presented to Lou. H. Silberman*, ed. J. L. Crenshaw and S. Sandmel (New York: KTAV, 1980), 143–63.

10. This is the good suggestion of Murray Baumgarten, editor of *Judaism*.

11. For a more detailed, academic study of Halivni's depth historiography, see Peter Ochs, "Talmudic Scholarship as Textual Reasoning: Halivni's Pragmatic Historiography," in *Textual Reasonings: Jewish Philosophy and Text Study at the End of the Twentieth Century*, ed. P. Ochs and N. Levene (Grand Rapids, MI: Eerdmans, 2003), 120–43.

1

Prayer in the Shoah

David Weiss Halivni

Editor's Introduction

Peter Ochs

David Halivni's "Prayer in the Shoah" offers one of the most significant testimonies on record of the theological consequences of the
Shoah: a wrenching, troubling, and yet tragically affirmative account
of what it means to have prayed in the camps and to pray again today. The context for this statement is comparably noteworthy. As
Halivni explains in the beginning of his essay, Yad Vashem asked him
to write the piece as an introduction to their publication of the High
Holiday Machzor used in the Wolfsberg concentration camp (and
transcribed for that purpose by the Satmar Hazan Naphtali Stern,
z"l). In correspondence, Halivni notes that he had been "looking for
quite a while for an opportunity to write about the mispairing of sin
and Holocaust. This may be the occasion, I thought, so I accepted the
invitation, even though I did not know at that time what the Sources
would show." He completed the essay just after Pesach 2000. Several
months later, just before Rosh Hashanah, Rabbi Obadiah Yosef, the
spiritual leader of Shas, spoke about the Shoah on his regular Satur-
day night sermon, broadcast over Israel radio. As Halivni recalls,
"Rabbi Yosef spoke of the connection between sin and suffering and
declared that the Holocaust was the result of sin and that the many
religious people who were killed in the Holocaust had been sinners
in a previous life (*gilgul*)." The radio show elicited powerful reactions
in the Israeli media. Except for support from the ultra-Orthodox

community, the report was generally condemned in various letters to the editor and in radio and television commentaries. When President Katsav of Israel criticized Rabbi Yosef's conclusion, members of Shas threatened the government. In January 2001, Halivni redelivered a version of the essay as a public lecture in Israel. He stressed three major themes of the essay you are about to read: the effort to associate the Shoah and sin is morally outrageous, it is unwarranted on a strict reading of the Tanakh, and it reinforces an alarming tendency among ultra-Orthodox leaders to exploit such arguments on behalf of their own authority.[1]

HALIVNI'S PERSONAL AND
THEOLOGICAL WITNESS TO THE SHOAH

Halivni spent his childhood in the Jewish community of Sighet, in the Carpathian Mountains. He was famous for his Talmudic erudition even as a child and even before his rabbinic ordination at the age of fifteen. But Hungarian Jewry had already begun to suffer the effects of Nazism several years before this, and, later that year, in 1944, he was deported, first to a ghetto, then to Auschwitz, later to the forced labor camp of Wolfsberg, in Gross-Rosen, then to the death camp of Ebensee. His family perished in Auschwitz, and he writes that, of his grandfather's sixty-five children, only five survived the camps. Inside the camps, he continued to teach Mishnah from memory until, as he recounts in his memoirs, the environment was no longer one into which he could open his mind to new levels of learning. He recalls,

> Even though I knew that the murderers were out there in the streets, . . . I shut them out, drew an imaginary wall and continued to do what I had done all those years, linking myself to the past and continuing to study the same material I had studied since the age of four. . . .
>
> That all changed on the fateful day of May 14, 1944. . . . We were told on that day that we had to leave our house . . . and wait in the street for transport. . . . At that time . . . I lost my home and my imaginary life stopped. I stopped learning . . . I had no desire or ability to study Torah amid people ready to kill us. I did not learn on the train and did not resume formal learning until months after liberation. . . .[2]
>
> In their wildest imagination the people of the ghetto could not have imagined what ultimately happened . . . that they would be gassed . . . including young children.[3]

Halivni's book of memoirs, *The Book and the Sword: A Life of Learning in the Shadow of Destruction* (1996), was composed and published more than fifty years after the horrible events that define them. The words and world of the Talmud had filled his imagination as a child. As a youth, they provided him a refuge ("an imaginary wall") from the horrible world around him. Through much of this adult life, they may have provided him a refuge as well from the memories of that world. But, in his memoirs, he describes one occasion on which this wall of imagination was breached: "I lost my home and my imaginary life stopped." It seems most prudent to understand his experience physiologically: "When physical survival itself was threatened, it was simply impossible to concentrate on book learning, even for the sake of refuge." Yet, his description of horrors that went beyond one's "wildest imagination" might also suggest something about the relation between Torah and imagination. If words of Torah can fill the entire imagination, can they also reach beyond the imagination? Or do events that shatter the imagination also threaten the universe of one's Torah learning? Is this, in fact, another way of characterizing the theological challenge that Halivni faced in writing his memoirs? Would the memory of such events also challenge the universe of one's Torah learning (and pierce the "wall of his imagination" a second time)? If so, we may wonder if "Prayer in the Shoah" offers Halivni's response to this broader challenge: a way, finally, to reimagine, rebuild, and renew the universe of Torah after the events of Shoah.

"Prayer in the Shoah" is what we may call a "theological testimony." It is, for one, written by a survivor of the Shoah and, in that sense, belongs to the literature of witness. But it is also a theological inquiry, composed by someone who is both a profound scholar of Talmudic literature and a rabbinic leader. Halivni's personal witness to the Shoah therefore, in a sense, brings a dimension of traditional rabbinic Judaism into the horrors of the Shoah and then out again. In the process, his witness enables the reader to see what it might mean for rabbinic Judaism itself to endure the Shoah and then persist again as rabbinic Judaism. How does the heart and soul of Talmudic Judaism suffer such an event? How does it withstand the event and not disintegrate in despair? How is it transformed through the event, so that what emerges into life after the Shoah is both traditional rabbinic Judaism *and* something else? And how does the transformation occur, in detail, to each aspect of rabbinic Judaism: its method of reading Torah, its sense of the Covenant between God and Israel, its understanding of sin and punishment, and its visions of God's relations to creation and, even, of God's self-relation?

Halivni may frustrate the tendency of many modern Jews to separate personal (or communal) from academic forms of writing. In both *Mekorot Umasorot* and his more general English writings, Halivni is careful to frame most of his work strictly within the limits of academic scholarship as most scholars define it today. He also offers a second level of inquiry, however, through which he entertains questions that cannot be answered within those limits. Even if these questions are not answered, he suggests, critical text scholars may survive or even prosper in their professions. But some of these questions speak to matters of life and death for the religion of Israel—for the spiritual, psychosocial, and corporate existence of Judaism after the Shoah. What, for example, is the status of the Covenant after the destruction of the Temple? Or after the Shoah?

Critical text scholars will surely acknowledge the importance of such questions to the practical lives of various rabbinic communities, and they may acknowledge the significant role of "mythmaking" in strengthening communal life—that is, the importance of "constructing narratives" that enable communities of Jews to give sense and order to their lives with one another. But most may assign *responsibility* for such "mythmaking" to "communal leaders" or to artists, sages, and composers. Leaders of traditional religious communities, on the other hand, will readily acknowledge the significance of such questions, but they may also claim that appropriate answers to them are available in the "tradition." Such leaders may then reaffirm the critical scholar's sense of a division of responsibility, but in reverse order: these questions are too important to be influenced by critical scholarship, and the responsibility for framing them must be left to appropriate religious authorities.

Halivni seeks both to acknowledge the separable spheres of critical and community-specific modes of study and, at the same time, to argue that both sides must give much more attention and care to a third mode of inquiry that falls in between them: what I previously labeled the "third direction" in recent Jewish scholarship.[4] For Halivni, what the critical scholar may label "mythmaking" is "made," to be sure, but *not only* by human hands. Furthermore, what the traditional religious leader says is "answered by tradition" is "inside" the tradition, to be sure, but cannot be brought to the light of day without human effort—and an effort that belongs to *this* day. His third mode of inquiry draws, at once, on both rabbinic leadership and critical inquiry, both traditional Torah learning and scientific study.

There are several ways of drawing these two sides into a single inquiry. One of Halivni's central approaches is to undertake religious historiography, or what we will label "depth historiography."[5] This is to encourage religiously committed academic scholars to conduct their scientific studies of historical evidence but then to contribute as well to their communities' wrestling with the "big questions" that exceed the limits of clear evidence. The first rule of depth historiography is to eliminate answers that would flatly contradict the evidence. The second rule is, among various possibilities, to select the one answer that responds to the community's sense of Torah by helping repair present-day crises in the community while at the same time reaffirming and extending the wisdoms of classical rabbinic Judaism. The third rule is that the capacity to make profound judgments of this kind requires prayer as well as critical rationality.

Halivni's essay illustrates another feature of his "third mode of inquiry." This is to write within the style and language of the medieval tradition of rabbinic commentary. While it is not obvious in the English translation, almost all of Halivni's text is written within the biblical, Talmudic, and Gaonic vocabularies typical of medieval commentaries: in both his textual citations (which you will see) and the paraphrases that are internal to his own sentences (which you may often not detect in the English). Halivni's text continually replays the medieval style, restating his main thesis each time it is demonstrated on yet another level of our textual heritage and re-citing illustrative sections of the *siddur,* or of the rabbinic and biblical literatures. In this way, he signals that his Jewish theology after the Shoah will remain deeply within the rabbinic tradition, reaffirming the biblical Covenant between God and Israel and traditional vocabularies of Bible, Talmud, and of post-Talmudic commentary. At the same time, by introducing the unsettling witness of the Shoah *into* these traditional vocabularies, he delivers the transformative consequences of the Shoah *into* the heart of rabbinic Judaism. In this way, he does not "add on" to the tradition but illustrates how it is relived today for this generation.

I believe Halivni understands himself to be writing in a way that is reassuring to an Orthodox readership, indicating that rabbinic Judaism lives on today, after the Shoah and without insulating itself from the religious consequences of the Shoah. At the same time, his writing also delivers an unsettling message: rabbinic Judaism may not be identical, today, to the religion promoted in the past three decades by Orthodox leaders and *roshe yeshivah*. He does not say this in the way such leaders may say they fear; that is, he does not diminish traditional rabbinic piety or *halakhah* or faith in the God of Israel. He suggests, instead, that for the people Israel after the Shoah, such piety may not be consistent with a number of claims made by Orthodox leaders today. The problem is not simply that these leaders may fail to speak Torah to the conditions of the day. It is, more gravely, that their anxieties about the changing face of our Covenant may have moved them to *reframe rabbinic Judaism as a system of unchanging doctrines and rules*—or *as a system of doctrines and rules that they alone are authorized to define for us, as if with direct divine commission.*

For Halivni, the deeper crisis is that, in the past three decades, such leaders have increasingly come to represent traditional Judaism and that *klal yisrael* therefore begins to identify "Jewish piety" with the orthodoxy of such leaders alone. The result is that both traditional and nontraditional Jews are led further away from the interpretive traditions of classical rabbinic Judaism. Traditional Jews are led away because they follow the examples of their leaders (whom they mistakenly identify with the methods of the classical sages); nontraditional Jews are led away because they flee from the same examples (which they also mistakenly identify with the methods of the classical sages).

WRITING AS REPAIRING

Halivni's writing works on several levels at once. On one level, "Prayer in the Shoah" is a personal testimony to the Shoah and to its impact on the beliefs of a survivor. On another level, it is a theodicy, an effort to account for the justness (or not) of God's actions in history: in this case to correct what he considers the deeply misguided theodicy offered by Rabbi Obadiah Yosef and by some other ultra-Orthodox leaders. The instrument of his theodicy is, on one level, plain-sense study of the biblical and rabbinic sources. What counts as "the Sins of Israel"? When and how does God punish such sins? Asking these questions of each of the classic sources, Halivni seeks to do his job not only as a text scholar but also as a religious mentor or rabbi: to offer interested readers scholarly grounds for answering personal religious questions. Is the Shoah punishment for Israel's sins? No, Halivni concludes;

if "sin" is to be defined in biblical terms, then there is plain-sense evidence that this utter destruction of many Jewish communities cannot result from sin. On another level, Halivni constructs his theodicy through a theosophy, an effort to narrate some aspect of the divine life about which we have no direct evidence. He makes clear to his readers that, on this level, he is writing not as a text scholar—offering evidence that should be of general interest to any student of the sources—but strictly as mentor or rabbi for believing Jews who would seek such guidance. He adapts and reimagines a version of the kabbalistic theosophy that Isaac Luria constructed in the shadow of the destruction of Spanish Jewry in the 16th century. In Halivni's version, God contracts into Himself (*metsimtsem*) in order to leave space for human freedom (to "leave a vacuum"), but the divine presence "leaks" back in over time (the "vacuum leaks"), bringing God closer at the cost of constricting human freedom to do good or evil. Taking note of this constriction, God reenacts His self-contraction (*tsimtsum*), restoring human freedom. Such events of contraction correspond, in earthly history, to times of maximal human freedom. Modern European history, Halivni surmises, may correspond to such a time, reaching a crescendo in the twentieth century, when humanity was most free to do as it pleased; as evidenced in the Shoah, it pleased to do evil.

What sense shall we make of such a theosophy? According to the "third way" of Jewish scholarship (see above), to examine and evaluate Halivni's construction is not to stand outside of time and "see what it really is" but to suggest *what effect* it would have in relation to each of one's different spheres of life and thought. We might, for example, ask how Halivni's theosophy would appear from the perspectives of each of the levels of Jewish study outlined in this book's introduction.

Plain sense: Halivni would argue, I believe, that while a Jewish theosophy must not contradict the plain sense of the biblical and rabbinic writings, the plain-sense allows for many possible theosophical constructions, of which his is one.

Depth historiography: On this level, we may ask which of these possible constructions would do two things: answer an urgent question we have about the plain sense that cannot be answered through the tools of plain sense science and thereby raise hypotheses of use to academic text scholarship. In our day, the urgent question is how to understand "the sins of Israel" in light of the Shoah. Halivni's first claim works within the bounds of academic depth historiography: one may reasonably conclude that the historical events of the Shoah do not fall within the domain of what the Bible and Talmud label "punishment for the sins of Israel." If read according to its own plain sense, however, Halivni's theosophical construction would appear to exceed the bounds of depth historiography. While his model of *tsimtsum* does not explicitly contradict the plain sense of Bible and Talmud, it does not appear to contribute to academic studies of Bible and Talmud. We would therefore evaluate this model as a contribution to explicitly *theological* inquiry alone.

Examined, however, from a different perspective, Halivni's theosophy may yield something of academic interest. We might classify his narrative of "cosmic vacuum and leakage" as a three-tiered reading of the biblical and rabbinic account of when and how Israel suffers. The first tier is his plain-sense reading: maximal suffering (as displayed in the destruction of whole communities of Jews) cannot be read as divine punishment. The second tier is his unstated yet implicit claim that the case of the Shoah also exceeds the bounds of the tradition's remaining accounts of suffering: for example, Isaiah's doctrine of Israel as "Suffering Servant," who suffers for the sins of the nations, or rabbinic accounts of the "Ten Martyrs," who suffered for the sake of sanctifying the divine name (*Eleh Ezkerah*). The third tier is Halivni's implicit claim—offered, by way of this imaginative narrative, for public rather than scholarly use—that this historical event may exceed the limits of biblical and rabbinic imagination. He has in this sense offered a religious-historical hypothesis about one limiting feature of biblical and rabbinic literatures: that they do not offer a way to name the ultimate negativity of the Shoah or to name actions that God cannot control (in the short run of human history) even if they threaten His very dominion on earth.[6] At the same time, he has offered another hypothesis about a deeper,[7] reparative dimension of these literatures: that they communicate their theological messages not only through what they name, portray, and represent but also through what they do, that is, through the way they stimulate and push us to read and interpret and act on what we interpret. This means that, on one level, these literatures draw a sharp distinction between what we can and cannot say and know of God: on this level, Halivni's witness to the Shoah exceeds what these literatures can portray and represent. On another level, however, the literatures draw a different distinction, between the realms of representation and of performance, so that what cannot be represented or portrayed *may yet be performed*.

In the specific case before us, this means that *although we cannot account in explicit words for how the God of Israel's Bible and Talmud can remain Israel's God after Auschwitz, we might read Halivni's activity of mythmaking as another, indirect way to demonstrate that the God of Israel remains the God of Israel nonetheless. The demonstration would appear not in the specific picture narrated in Halivni's theosophy but in the faith, passion, commitment, imagination, sad realism, persistent hope, prior reading, present unreading, and future rereading displayed in the activity that generated his narrative. For Halivni, all these characteristics are the fruit of Torah study alone: the dimension of Torah study that is disclosed when (and perhaps only when) the events of this life far exceed the limits of the plain sense of Bible and Talmud.*

The Shoah is not the only event of this kind. In the desert, for example, or in each new code of law, in each prophecy, in the life of Job and the work of Ezra, the Bible narrates new ways of enacting Torah that accompany events even less dramatic than the Exodus and the Destruction of the Temple.[8] In the shadow of the Second Destruction, the Mishnah displays a language of Torah that appears at times to have no precedent within the biblical literature. And post-Talmudic writings are replete with subsequent examples of what David Roskies terms the Jewish "literatures of destruction," from Isaac's Luria's writings after the Expulsion from Spain to the words of the Baal Shem Tov after the Chmielnicki's pogroms to early Zionist responses to the pogroms of czarist Russia. Halivni argues, nevertheless, that the Shoah is unique among such events, unique in the degree to which it exhausts the narrative (or representational) capacity of all prior Jewish literature. Why does this not therefore lead him to abandon that literature and its attendant faith? *Because this ultimate test challenges the literatures of Torah to display their ultimate power: "revelation," understood as the power to reorient Israel toward God's presence amidst the failures of any inherited means of representing that presence. As displayed in this book's prologue and epilogue, Halivni believes there are two defining revelations of this kind in Israel's history: Sinai and Auschwitz.*

Theological writing: Halivni's narrative is also "theology," by which we mean writing addressed to specific communities of Jews to help them maintain lives of Torah when historical events contradict their plain-sense understanding of the classic sources and the traditions that transmit them. If read in terms of some Talmudists' strict dichotomy between legal interpretation and *aggadah* (theological narration or storytelling), Halivni's narrative may appear as "mere narrative," an effort to serve our need for belief but not our need to understand what the world really is and how we should act in it. In terms of Halivni's "third way" of writing, however, this narrative represents what we might call merely the "jacket cover" of a book of injunction and practical instruction. The story of cosmic contraction and "leakage" may be read as the believer's entrée into a frightening confrontation with God's seeming incapacity to draw near. That confrontation may, in turn, be experienced as generating a series of new religious directives, including these:

- *Do not cover over.* As introduced in the next chapter, "Restoring Scripture," this is a dominant lesson of Halivni's Talmudic science: do not presume that a text is less sacred if it displays inner contradictions, apparent errors, or "blemishes" (*pegamim*). When you come across such a text, do not seek therefore to *cover over* its blemishes with *forced interpretations* (*dechukim*) that replace what is ugly, confusing, or frightening with what appears smooth and rational. According to "Prayer in the Shoah," this lesson for reading sacred texts is also a lesson for reading history: do not cover over the fact of Shoah or its implications for belief and for reason. Do not, therefore, preserve your customary practice of faith at the expense of covering over what flatly contradicts it. Do not, at the same time, preserve your customary practice of reason as if it somehow could account for what faith cannot. Do not even preserve your customary practice of keeping silent before what you cannot comprehend, as if the only goal of speech were comprehension.
- *Act in the face of what is frightening and unfathomable. Act to repair and to restore.* This is, once again, first and foremost a directive for Talmud study. Halivni's primary work in *Mekorot Umasorot* is to look behind the Talmud's forced interpretations to reconstruct whatever contradictions and blemishes they may have covered over and then to propose ways of both resolving them (if possible) and of living with them. I believe some scholars misinterpret Halivni's work when they assume his goal is only the literal one of recovering a textual "source" that may be lost behind subsequent editings. His devotion to the work of "restoration" is so comprehensive that I believe it constitutes a religious devotion, or one that has no finite limit. The goal, in other words, is to restore not merely the textual sources but also all the sources of these sources, to restore the words of revelation as they are spo-

ken. Since these are not finite goals, I must assume he adopts them as a means of participating in the infinite life. But this does not mean to rest with the image of the infinite as some realm free, finally, from these blemishes. He cannot now imagine anything without imagining blemish and, therefore, without the imagination's prompting him to work for restoration. God alone is infinite, but the infinite is also a place of work for restoration. So, he reminds us in this essay that, in the Rabbis' understanding, God also prays, praying that His attribute of mercy will restrain His attribute of justice. And what does He now pray? Halivni surmises that He must pray that all human beings use their freedom for the good and, in this way, strengthen His attribute of mercy.

- *Pursue science and prayer.* The most important science is the scientific pursuit of the plain sense of Talmud and Torah. The most important prayer is for God to rule over us all again, "Rule over all the world in your full glory" (*m'loch al kol ha'olam b'khvodekha*). These are Halivni's two primary directives for action after the Shoah, for the sake of contributing to Israel's potential movement from Auschwitz back to Sinai.

NOTES

An earlier version of this introduction was published as "Introduction to David Weiss Halivni's 'Prayer in the Shoah,'" in *Judaism* 199, vol. 50, no. 3 (summer 2001): 259–67. Our thanks to *Judaism* editor Murray Baumgarten for his encouragement and guidance.

1. Some leaders even claimed, for example, that their yeshivot represent the true tradition of Torah since they survived the Shoah and must therefore have been free of sin.

2. David Weiss Halivni, *The Book and the Sword: A Life of Learning in the Shadow of Destruction* (Boulder, CO: Westview Press: 1998), 46–47.

3. Halivni, *The Book*, 55–57.

4. See the introduction to this book, pp. 6ff, where I suggest that Halivni's work shares in a new direction in Jewish scholarship that follows neither the rationalist nor radically skeptical alternatives in modern scholarship.

5. In *Revelation Restored*, Halivni labels this "transcendent history"; in my preface to his book, I relabel it "depth historiography," as distinguished from the "plain-sense historiography" of historical science. Murray Baumgarten, editor of *Judaism*, thoughtfully suggested the term "religious historiography,"

and we agreed to use it when this essay appeared in *Judaism*. While "religious historiography" displays more clearly the general force of this kind of inquiry, I use here the uglier term "depth historiography" in order to leave room for many other forms of "depth"—which could also be drawn, for example, from wisdom traditions, personal self-reflection, psychoanalysis, and so on.

6. Such insights may also be drawn from the long history of what David Roskies calls the "literatures of destruction" in Judaism. See his collection *The Literature of Destruction: Jewish Responses to Catastrophe* (Philadelphia: Jewish Publication Society, 1992).

7. "Deeper," in the sense of one's deepest presuppositions, which can be brought to awareness only through searing interruptions in one's everyday life and, even then, only through unusually penetrating practices of reflection.

8. See, for example, Michael Fishbane, *Biblical Interpretation in Ancient Israel* (Oxford: Oxford University Press, 1985), 337ff., 361ff., 392ff.

Prayer in the Shoah

This essay was prepared as a meditation to accompany the prayer book *Machzor Wolfsberg*, published by Yad Vashem. The Machzor contains High Holiday prayers transcribed from memory by the Satmar Hazan Naphtali Stern, z"l, in 1945, in preparation for the Rosh Hashanah service he was about to lead in the Wolfsberg Labor Camp. (Hazan Stern recounts that he wrote the prayers "in pen, on paper torn from cement bags that I purchased [at great risk to his own life] in exchange for bread." Since then, "for forty three years, the pages were always stored in [my family] Machzor.") When Stern decided to give the pages to Yad Vashem for safekeeping, he broke out in tears, kissed them, and said, "I made a supreme effort to safeguard these. I did not know then, in the camp, that these writings would become a national treasure. God willing, they will remain before my eyes on Rosh Hashanah."[1] I, too, was an inmate in Wolfsberg, and I remember the prayer service. The service was held in an overcrowded hall, and—still a young man of sixteen—I could not push my way in and remained outside. But what went on inside left a deep impression. This was the only time that we were permitted to gather together in the camp and pray out loud. The prayers that were uttered that day were the traditional ones, composed in a different age and under very different conditions. Nevertheless, among the traditional prayers, one was uttered as a prayer of the heart with a unique *kavanah*, unique to the incomparable conditions of the prayers. This essay is a meditation on that prayer.

There is no society without worshippers,
There is no time without someone who prays,
There is no place that cannot be transformed into a place of prayer
And there is no human being who does not, in the privacy of his heart,
embrace a silent prayer, offered up to the hidden powers, to redeem him
from his distress,
To improve his condition and to better his lot.
The human being is a being who prays

Prayer is individual; each person has his own prayer. The sages, to be sure, canonized Jewish prayer and prohibited any changes in it. On the one hand, this prohibition made rabbinic prayer publicly recognizable, so that worshippers would feel at home in every synagogue they entered and could participate in every prayer they heard. On the other hand, the prohibition increased the risk that rabbinic prayer might become routine.

Even when prayers are similar in content, they differ in the amount of emphasis, enthusiasm, and heartbreak that should accompany them. The worshipper's mood determines the intensity and devotion (*devekut*) of prayer, and this changes from day to day and hour to hour. No one prays with the same intentionality (*kavanah*) on two different occasions, just as no one enters precisely the same body of water on two occasions. The restlessness of the human heart releases feelings that stimulate ever new intentionalities of prayer. No two people, therefore, pray with the same intentionality, just as no two people experience the same mood. Although the Rabbinic tradition of prayer is fixed, the accompaniments of prayer change from person to person and from time to time. This is how it always was, and this is how it was in the camps.

If we are, therefore, to assess what prayer uniquely characterized prayer in the labor camps, we should not search for some new prayer. Beside our reluctance to change prayers, particularly on the High Holidays, the torture and fear that prevailed in the concentration camps and forced labor camps silenced the creative urge. We should also not expect to find some particular, traditional prayer that became a favorite to most of the worshippers in the camps. Most worshippers simply prayed according to their usual manner and custom. Only a very few, exceptional individuals, aware of their terrible circumstances, understood the substance and significance of the words of prayer and were sensitive to the theological problems entailed in their being uttered in that place. They sought some traditional prayer that would express their deep longing to overcome the forces arrayed against them, and their sense that the suffering and misery around them was the result of satanic, cosmic forces over which they had no control or influence. They found such a prayer in the prayer *"eloheinu v'elohei avotenu m'lokh al kol ha'olam b'khvodekha . . .":* "Our God and God of our ancestors, reign over all the world in your full glory. . . ." In this prayer, which belongs to the Amidah for Rosh Hashanah, we ask God to reign alone, to take the reins in his hands and not allow these satanic forces to prevail.

To understand the full meaning of this prayer, we must first reflect deeply on the question that grounds all Holocaust theology: *Do we attribute the Shoah to sin?* Lest there be any doubt about my own response to this question, I will state my conclusions at the outset. *It is written in the Torah, a second time in the Prophets, a third time in the Writings, and a fourth time in the words of our sages, that the Shoah was not the consequence of sin.*

"IT WAS WRITTEN IN THE TORAH"—WHERE?

"And yet for all that, when they are in the land of their enemies, I will not cast them away, nor will I loathe them, to destroy them utterly, and to break my covenant with them" (Leviticus 26:44). After the Torah warns the children of Israel that, if they sin they will be driven out of their land and suffer disease, war, and famine (to the point of eating human flesh), it closes with the assurance that, despite their sins, God will not despise or reject or annihilate them (*yavi otam l'khilayon*) and will not abrogate the covenant that he swore to Abraham, Isaac, and Jacob. *According to the covenant made between God and Israel, they would not be destroyed for their sins.*

What does the word *l'khalotam*, "to annihilate them," mean? Should we understand this in a quantitative or qualitative sense? Does it mean that He will not *completely* destroy them—to the point that not even a survivor or refugee is left—or that He will not destroy to such an extent that they cannot rebuild their lives? Those who claim that the Shoah is a result of sin will interpret *l'khalotam* quantitatively, as total annihilation, total extermination. From this perspective, if any survivor remained, then, even though most of the population was destroyed, this would not count as "total annihilation" and would not therefore weaken God's promise to Israel. These interpreters believe that since there were survivors who rebuilt their lives and also contributed to the enhancement of Judaism—even though very few Jews from Eastern Europe survived—a small part of the promise must have been kept. In this view, those who were destroyed were punished for their sins. These interpreters, therefore, believe that the Shoah was a consequence of sin. *This interpretation is incorrect and misguided.*

L'khalotam does not mean total extermination,[2] the killing of a people or a large part of it, but rather the irremediable destruction of a people's institutional infrastructure. And this is precisely what happened in the Shoah: institutional Jewish life in Eastern Europe was uprooted and almost totally erased; the only survivors were as brands snatched from the fire. The limits of *lo l'khalotam* were blurred and suspended, and the covenant God made with Israel was shaken if not totally abrogated. *We cannot, therefore, attribute the Shoah to sin.* God promised not to destroy Israel for their sins, and there is no greater destruction in history than the Shoah.

As for the kinds of destruction that God might bring as a punishment for sin: this could result in the people's being exiled to a foreign land, as characterized in the first Rebuke (*tokhecha*) in *parashat bechukotai* (Leviticus 26). Or, this kind of destruction could result in the people's being conquered while on in their own soil, as characterized in the second Rebuke in *parashat ki tavo* (Deuteronomy 28). In both cases, individuals die from disease, war, famine, and other causes.[3]

We must bear in mind that the relationship between destruction and sin is different from the relationship between exile and sin. On several occasions, the Torah takes note of the relationship between exile and sin and even offers the following reason for it. The people who first inhabited the Land were expelled and killed because of their abominations. The Torah was, therefore, concerned to specify what these abominations were in minute detail, so that the Children of Israel would be clearly warned: if they, too, turned toward these abominations, they would have no more right than their predecessors to remain in the Land. Like the first inhabitants, they too would be expelled. In the language of the Torah, "the country will vomit them out." "Do not defile yourselves in any of these ways," so that "the land will not vomit you out the way it vomited out the nation that came before you" (Leviticus 18:28 and 20:22). There is therefore legal justification for the belief that "We were exiled from our land on account of our sins" (*mipnei chatotenu galinu me'artsenu*).

But there is no justification for relating *khilayon* ("annihilation") to sin. The Holy One promised Israel that, even if they were in the land of their enemies, He would not annihilate them or destroy their capacities to reorganize their lives and return to their land. When their land was conquered, He promised to remove the yoke of the nations from their necks so that they might reestablish themselves. In our own age, most of the edifice of Judaism has been destroyed beyond repair by the cruelest actions in human history. We must not blame such a catastrophe on the sins of its victims. Anyone who does so denies the promises God made to Israel and merits our careful scrutiny (*"v't-sarikh l'vdok acharov . . ."*).

"IT WAS WRITTEN IN THE PROPHETS?"—WHERE?

In the Torah, the proof for our thesis can be found only by analyzing the word *l'khalotam* ("to annihilate you"). In the Prophets, especially the book of Jeremiah, the evidence is clear and precise. I will cite and interpret only the primary prooftexts: Jeremiah's prayer in chapter 10:24: "Chastise me, O Lord, but in measure, not according to Your anger, lest You reduce me to nothing"; and God's promise in chapters 30:11 and 46:28: "For I am with you to deliver you, declares the Lord. I will make an end of all the nations among which I have dispersed you. But I will not make an end of you. I will not leave you unpunished, but I will chastise you in measure." Jeremiah prays that, while chastising Israel for their sins, God will chastise them "only in measure," which Radak interprets as "as much as we can suffer," according to our capacities. Individuals will suffer disease, war, famine, and other deaths, but the "doorposts" (*amot hasipim*) will not be moved, and the bases for everyday existence will not be undone. Communal activities will continue, even if in terrible suffering—but without destruction. This point is emphasized again in the words *al be'apekha*, "Do not act out of Your wrath," please, do not be angry, *pen yamitenu* "lest we die," lest we would be annihilated, *tihe keliyah*. In Radak's reading, "if You chastise us in anger, You will reduce us to something less than a people" (*im teyasveni be'apkha, tam'itenu mi l'heyot goy*). But if You chastise us in measure, we will remain a people: our corporate life will continue even after Your chastisement.

Jeremiah's prayer was accepted, and, in chapters 30:11 and 46:28, the Holy One promises Israel, "I will indeed chastise you in measure and will not utterly destroy you." In Radak's reading, "I will chastise you in proportion to what you can tolerate, not in proportion to my anger and fury, and not in proportion to your evil deeds." That is to say, your evil deeds merit your annihilation, but our God is a god of compassion and mercy and would not inflict total destruction. Radak offers this evidently ancient reading from Targum Yonatan, which reads, "You will suffer God's chastisements, but will be spared the full extent of the law" (chapter 10)—that is, you will be spared annihilation. The Targum adds, in chapter 30, "You will suffer chastisements for the sake of instruction, but you will be spared the full extent of the law. The Targum adds l'alfutekha—"to teach you"—and Rashi adds me'at me'at ("little by little"). Both Rashi and the Targum thus extend the meaning of the word l'mishpat ("in measure") in order to indicate that the chastisements will not be too strong. This says explicitly that the Holy One will chastise Israel in proportion to their sins but will not annihilate them. The Holy One gave this promise only to Israel. As for individuals, while they may suffer death, they may also avert the decree through repentance, prayers, and charity, although there is no promise that these will succeed.[4]

What happened in the Shoah is above and beyond measure (l'mishpat): above and beyond suffering, above and beyond any punishment. There is no transgression that merits such punishment. Such utter destruction has never transpired before in history, has never before been fashioned by Satan, and it cannot be attributed to sin. Whoever attributes the Shoah to sin denies the promise God made on two occasions to the prophet Jeremiah: "with respect to you" (itkha)—the people Israel—"I will not bring annihilation and will not utterly destroy" (lo eese khale venake lo anakekha). Such a person not only accuses the sufferers slanderously with having caused their own suffering but also indirectly belittles the guilt of the truly guilty by implying that they only did what they had to do. If not they, then some others would have had to do this. Such things must not be uttered!

I cannot fail to take note of the texts that appear to contradict my claim that sins do not bring annihilation. Most texts that appear to contradict my reading of khala are easily reconciled by noting that, in these texts, khala does not apply to all Israel or even most of Israel but only to individuals and groups who are not included in the promise that God made "not to annihilate them." Among such texts are Jeremiah 9:15, "I will send the sword after them until I have consumed them"; Jeremiah 14:12, "I will consume them by the sword, by famine, and by disease"; and Ezekiel 5:13, "I will vent my fury on them." One case is, however, difficult to reconcile in this way: Jeremiah's prophecy on "the Remnant of Judah" (*sh'erit yehuda*) in Jeremiah 42:44. The difficulty gets stronger when we see that the sources there are contradictory and that the matter belongs among God's secrets, *behadi k'vshi drachmana* (*Hagigah* 13a, Berakhot 10a). Let us therefore consider the matter at length.

In chapter 44:12–14, Jeremiah prophesies about the Remnant of Judah in Egypt: "In the land of Egypt, they will fall by the sword, they will be consumed by famine, young and old alike they will die by sword and famine. . . . Of the remnant of Judah who came to live in Egypt, no survivor or fugitive will be left. . . ." Only refugees will return, and all this destruction comes "Because you burned incense and poured libations to the Queen of Heaven," "And because you sinned against the Lord and did not listen to His voice" (44:23). Jeremiah prophesies that, because of their sins, "all the men of Judah will perish . . . in Egypt." This source might appear to contradict my claim that the Holy One promised not to destroy even a large part of Israel. My response is that the Remnant of Judah was then a small group: a few people who asked Jeremiah to pray for them. They said, "We remain a few of many" (42:20). They chose a perverse path and, against their own vital interests, decided not to stay in the country and accept Babylonian rule. Rejecting the prophet's promise that the Babylonians would pity them and return them to their land, they escaped to Egypt at the very time it was about to fall to Nebuchadnezzar.[5] They did so only through their obstinate belief that going to Egypt would enable them to continue their idol worship: "to burn incense and pour libations to the Queen of Heaven." They complained that only this idol worship would save them from calamity: "Ever since we stopped making offerings to the Queen of Heaven and pouring libations to her we have lacked everything and have been consumed by sword and famine" (44:18). "Going to Egypt" thus became a symbol of the strength of idol worship, and this is what Jeremiah tried to prevent with all the prophetic powers he possessed.

The center of public institutional and creative life was then in the Captivity, by the River Chebar. For the thirty years that they were there (Jehoiachin's exile was in 597 B.C.E.), the exiles strengthened and expanded their communal life. There Ezekiel prophesied. There the people mourned when they heard of the destruction of the Temple (Ezekiel 7), and there they built houses, planted vineyards, and sought, through prayer and synagogue life, to find a temporary substitute for Temple service. At the same time, the Remnant of Judah withered like an atrophied limb on the Jewish body: cut off from the rest of the exiles, isolated, and drawn toward idol worship. All this, despite the prophet's frequent warnings that they would suffer the same fate as the inhabitants of Jerusalem and the cities of Judah, who were completely destroyed. They did not listen and as a result suffered an even more devastating fate, and nothing remained of them. They were judged as individual idolaters or as members of "a city condemned for idolatry" (*ir hanidachat*), and therefore God's promises did not apply to them.[6]

According to Josephus (*Antiquities* 10.9.7), and according to Rabbi Joseph Karo's commentary on Jeremiah 44:14 (citing *Seder Olam*), some of the Remnant of Judah survived when Nebuchadnezzar captured Egypt and took the Jews of Egypt captive.[7] For this reason, we cannot compare what happened to the Remnant of Judah with what happened in our generation. The martyrs murdered in the Shoah represented the backbone of the Jewish people. Although not all of them were believers, all of them rejected paganism, and the sages said, long ago, "Whoever rejects idolatry is judged as one who affirmed the whole Torah" (*Hullin* 5a).

"IT WAS WRITTEN IN THE WRITINGS"—WHERE?

Within the *Writings*, we will focus primarily on Nehemiah 9. In this chapter, the author offers a historical survey, from the creation of heaven and earth ("You made the heavens, the highest heavens, the earth and everything that is on it," 9:6) until his own day ("Here we are today," 9:36). Briskly and clearly, he summarizes the miracles that God performed for Israel, the commandments, the ordinances, and the Torah that God commanded them, and also the people's obstinacy in rejecting His commandments and abandoning His Torah. God punished them and delivered them to their enemies: "Their enemies oppressed them. In their time of trouble, they cried to You and You heard them from heaven" (9:27); "But after they had rest from their troubles, they again committed evils before you . . . and You heard them from heaven and rescued them out of Your great compassion, again and again" (9:28). He saves them despite their sins and their insolence because He is "gracious and merciful, long-suffering, and of great kindness" (9:17). Despite their sins and their insolence, He refrained from destroying them (*l'khalotam*), even when their "iniquities are overwhelming." Five times, the author restates that out of His great mercy, God did not abandon them but saved them in times of trouble. He stresses, moreover, that "Out of Your great compassion, You did not destroy them or abandon them, for You are a gracious and compassionate god" (9:31). They deserved to be destroyed, but He spared them out of His great mercy and refrained from utterly destroying them.

The way Nehemiah 9 employs the term *khala* implies that, in other places in the Bible as well, the term *khala* does not refer to complete annihilation. In the promise, "I will not utterly destroy you" (*lo eese khala*), *khala* does not refer to the literal annihilation of all Israel but to the irremediable destruction of Israel's institutional foundations. It is absurd to associate the attributes of the One who is merciful and compassionate with the destruction of a major part of the people. Individuals or even small groups may suffer death, but *klal yisrael* remains and is slowly rebuilt; or, if exiled, it is eventually returned to its land. This was God's promise to Jeremiah, and this was the reason Nehemiah spoke of God's attributes of mercy and compassion. *In His great mercies He saves Israel from the threshold of destruction.*[8]

"IT WAS WRITTEN IN THE
RABBINIC LITERATURE"—WHERE?

Let us return to the rebuke in Leviticus 26 about which we opened our discussion of the Torah. Numbered among the curses are three that would appear, on a literal reading, to speak of *kaliah*, total destruction: "I will scatter you among the nations, and I will unsheath the sword against you" (26:33), and "You will perish among the nations, and the land of your enemies will consume you" (26:38). God, in other words, will disperse you among the nations, among whom you will be assimilated, and the "land"—that is, the peoples living on the land—will utterly consume you. The sages explained these curses differently, however. For the *Mekhilta*, "I will scatter you" (*etkhem ezereh*) does not mean "I will annihilate you" but, rather, "you will not be exiled in only one place"—since, "when the people of one country are exiled to a single place, they can see each other and are therefore consoled. But you will not be treated so." You will be dispersed so far apart from one another that you will be unable to see each other and ease the suffering. *You will suffer,* therefore, *but you will also live*; you will not be in danger of extinction.

Rashi offers a similar interpretation, reading "You will perish among the nations" (*veavadaten bagoyim*)[9] to mean that "you will be lost" rather than "annihilated." "When you are dispersed you will be 'lost to' (distant from) each other," and you will not enjoy the help and consolation that members of a group provide each other. Ibn Ezra interprets the end of the verse—"the land will consume you" (*ve'akhla etkhem*)—in the same spirit: that is, "most of those who are exiled to a new place tend to die from the change of climate and water" (but not literally "most" since, except for those with stomach or lung problems, most people will get used to the new climate). Thus, Ibn Ezra also interprets *kaliah* ("total destruction") to mean "the death of many individuals" rather than literal "annihilation." In his commentary on Rashi, Rabbi Eliyahu Mizrachi claims that Rashi—and one could also add Ibn Ezra and the *Mekhilta*—would explain that "the exiles would not literally perish, since, if so, how would God maintain His promise? Instead, God assures them that, even when they are in the land of their enemies, He will not despise them so much that they would perish."

These commentators interpret *l'khalotam,* as we have suggested earlier in our discussion, as referring to the promise that God will not "destroy the community of Israel beyond repair." Had they, indeed, interpreted it to mean that God will not "utterly destroy Israel," then they would have read the three curses according to their apparently literal meaning. In this case, "I will scatter you among the nations," "you will be lost among the nations," and "the land of your enemies will consume you" would all refer to *khaliah* as "utter destruction." Even though these commentators do not mention Jeremiah's prayer (in 10:24) and God's promise not to destroy Israel (in 30:10; 46:29), this prayer and this promise must have been on their minds when they offered their interpretation. This prayer and promise also needs to be kept today as a sign and a warning not to attribute the Shoah to sin. *There is no sin or transgression that merits a punishment like the Shoah.*

Everything I have said so far concerns *klal yisrael*: that Israel would not be destroyed as a collectivity. Individuals may, however, still die from their transgressions, whether punished by heaven or by humans (by the courts). This matter is very complicated, and I raise it only to explain that all Israel, or most of its foundations, will not be destroyed, even when it has filled its full measure of sin. The Talmud

(*Shabbat 55a*) has a difference of opinion about whether individuals suffer the punishment of death even when they do not sin. (I will not at this time discuss the corresponding argument in the Book of Job since it is of a different type.) Rabbi Ami[10] determines that "there is no death without sin and no suffering without transgression." The Gemara argues, however, based on a Baraita,[11] that there is death without sin, and from that we may deduce that there is also suffering without transgression.[12] If this were a halakhic argument, then certainly all the decisors would judge according to the Baraita,[13] particularly after the Gemara closes by affirming that "the refutation of Rav Ami stands."[14] Since, however, this is a nonhalakhic argument (in which case one is not required to follow the received opinion of the Gemara), it is possible to follow one of the minority opinions, even one that was rejected.[15]

For this reason, some of the Rishonim—especially those with philosophic approaches, like the Rambam and the Meiri—abandoned the conclusion of the Gemara and were drawn to Rav Ami's idea that there is no death without sin and no suffering without transgression. They were captivated by the philosophically more convincing and eloquent saying that "God does not withhold the reward of any creature" (*Pesachim* 118a, *Baba Kamma* 38b) and does not punish people who have not brought it on themselves. The Rambam argues this way, for example, in the *Guide for the Perplexed* (III:17 p. 311). After summarizing the five opinions that people appear to hold about Providence, he says, "We believe that Providence always brings human beings what they deserve, and far be it from God to punish anyone who was not deserving. . . . And almost all of our sages say clearly that there is no death without sin and no suffering without transgression." Similarly, after bringing the opinion of the multitude "that God brings suffering independently of sin," the Rambam says that "the principle of Torah that runs counter to this opinion is contained in His dictum, may He be exalted, 'A God of faithfulness and without iniquity.' Nor do all the sages share this opinion of the multitude, since they said, long ago, 'There is no death without sin and no suffering without transgression.' And this is the opinion that ought to be followed by all Torah scholars endowed with intellect, for they should not ascribe injustice to God" (in III:24 p. 329). There is a hint here that the saying—"God does not withhold the reward of any creature"—remains controversial,[16] but, in any event, the Rambam disregards the Gemara's refutation.

Unlike the Rambam, Rav Menachem Hameiri does not disregard the Gemara's refutation; he cites it and then seeks to invalidate it:

> The essence of religion is to believe that God oversees everything that happens, from good to evil, and does not withhold the reward of any creature, for better or worse. Thus it is said that there is no death without sin and no punishment without transgression. . . . Even though the Gemara retained another view in its refutation, the principles of faith do not depend on the testimony of the plain sense of Scripture and of Aggadah. And it is well known that we do not base refutations on Aggadot. (Bet Habechira on *Shabbat* 55b)

The Meiri not only rejects the Gemara's refutation (he considers the Baraita a merely popular Aggadah) but also establishes a general principle: the essence of faith should be based not on "the plain sense of Scripture and Aggadah" but, rather, on that inquiry and deliberation that emerge from Scriptures and, perhaps, the Aggadot. This is, in fact, a fundamental principle of medieval Jewish philosophy, serving as well as a guide to textual exegesis: how to relate to the text, what to take from it and what not.

We cannot determine whether these philosophic exegetes apply their retributive doctrine of "no sin without punishment and no punishment without sin" to *klal yisrael* or only to individuals. Do they read God's promise to the prophet Jeremiah (not to destroy Israel even when their crimes require it) as a denial of the doctrine that God does not withhold the reward of any creature, for better or worse? Or do they believe that God treats *klal yisrael* differently—bestowing unmerited favor on them as a part of the covenant He made with Abraham, Isaac, and Jacob? It is hard to prove either reading from the Scriptural verses, since the Rambam and the Meiri are not interested in the "external (or plain) meanings of the Tanakh," while we put all our trust in the plain sense of the text—which shows that Israel, or a large part of Israel, may indeed sin without appropriate punishment.

Since the Shoah must not be seen as a consequence of sin, we conclude that it remains an unsolved enigma. Whoever seeks to explain the Shoah reduces it to some natural phenomena, belittles its evil, and assuages the guilt of those who perpetrated it. Nevertheless, we need to find an appropriate metaphor to express our understanding that the victims had no part in their own suffering and that nothing they had done or not done would have altered the constellation of their sufferings. The Shoah came upon them as a result of cosmolog-

ical forces that collided and struggled with each other and thus struck
the apple of the eye of history—the people of Israel. We turn to this
theme in the second part of our discussion.

TEN MEASURES OF EVIL DESCENDED INTO THE WORLD. NINE WERE TAKEN BY OUR GENERATION, AND ONE BY THE REST OF HISTORY.

In the previous section, we grounded our argument in God's promise
to Jeremiah that He will not utterly destroy Israel because of their sins:
v'nakeh lo anakekha. On the basis of this promise, we concluded that
what happened to us in our generation was not a consequence of our
sins. It was not because of their sins that toddlers and babies suffocated in gas chambers. They suffocated because human evil reached its
pinnacle in our time.

Human history is rich in wickedness, malice, and crime. But our
generation exceeds all its predecessors in its cruelty: in its malicious
determination to destroy everything that was Jewish and through the
cruelest means and by use of the most powerful forces. My heart stops
when I read comparisons between the Shoah and anything that happened before it. There are those—including the most respected and
influential Holocaust theologians—who see only a quantitative difference between the Shoah, the crusades, the inquisition, and the per-
secution and slaughter of the Jews under Chmielnicki in 1648–49.
They see only a matter of numbers. But this not right since in all these
cases Jews could have saved themselves had they been willing to convert, even in the slaughter of 1648–49. The killers thought they were
raising the souls of their victims to a higher plane, that what they were
doing was for their own good, to save them from worse suffering in
the next world. Their crushing hatred was not primarily against Israel
as a people or a race but against its religion. Those who accepted
Christianity were released. But, in our generation, the Jews had no way
out. Whoever was born Jewish or was of Jewish descent was condemned to be executed, and nothing could change the decree. This
should not be taken lightly. During the previous persecutions, the sufferers found solace in the belief that they were dying as martyrs. There
was no such solace for most of those slaughtered in our generation—
and among them were those who endured heart-wrenching despair
because they could find no meaning and value in their suffering.

All this and more. It is estimated that, in one week in Auschwitz, more Jews died, through a terrible variety of deaths, than in all the previous persecutions put together. The quantitative difference is so great that the difference in quantity itself becomes a difference in quality. We read in Lamentations, "Little children begged for bread" (4:4); in Auschwitz, Maidenek, and the other death camps, there were no little children. They were gassed. The destruction and devastation that comes in the wake of such massive killing undermines the very foundations of public life. When there are as yet only a few victims of such murder, corporate life continues to function; but the difference between a small number of victims and a very large number is the difference between life for the people as a whole and death.

Beyond any comparisons between the Shoah and various pogroms, I also reject any comparisons between the Shoah and both the First and Second Destructions of the Temple. The Shoah surpasses them in cruelty, hatred, and the magnitude of destruction. I am not referring to spiritual life. The Destruction of the First Temple initiated religious transformations that would continue for generations. It led to a process of religious decentralization that resulted in the growth of synagogues and in the emergence of new sources of religious authority. Responsibility for administering religious life was handed over from a select few—the Kohanim and Levi'im, whose positions were hereditary and who performed their functions only at certain set times of prayer, on Sabbaths and Holidays—to the people Israel as a whole—to every individual, whose prayers were offered every day and all times of the year.

The conditions after the Destruction of the Second Temple were different. To be sure, the center of religious life—the Temple—was destroyed, and sacrificial services were discontinued. But it is not clear that the Destruction led to a general impoverishment of spiritual life. Most of the Kohanim belonged to the Sadducean party and conducted their rituals according to Sadducean custom, despite the objections of the sages—who applied to some of them the verse of Proverbs 10:7, "The name of the wicked will rot" (*Mishnah Yoma*, 3:11). Furthermore, during the Second Temple period, the Beth Midrash, the center of both midrash and Mishnah, entered into serious competition with the Temple. Through *talmud torah*, the study of Torah, a person could feel close to God even without entering the Temple and without offering sacrifices. The Beth Midrash, moreover, was open to people from all classes of society and not only to the aristocracy.

Even though the Amoraim living in the land of Israel longed for the Temple and enacted several laws and ordinances "in memory of the Temple" (*zekher l'mikdash*), it is noteworthy that the Palestinian sources do not include the kind of statement that we find in the Babylonian Talmud (for example, in *Betsah* 5b): "The Temple may soon be rebuilt, and people would say, did we do so last year or not. . . ? Now, too, let us do so or not. . . ." In place of such a statement, the Palestinian Amoraim use the phrase "in memory of the Temple," which gives the impression that they had already abandoned hope and that nothing more remained of the Temple than memories. To declare, however, that "The Temple will speedily be rebuilt" is to share one's hope that it *will* very soon be rebuilt (and, when this happens, the people will remember how differently they behaved the year before). Distant from the events of the Destruction in time and place, the Babylonian Amoraim reflected nostalgically on the possibility of rebuilding the Temple, while those who lived in the land of Israel, closer to the events, understood the situation more realistically. Within the tannaitic literature, unlike the prophetic literature, it is difficult to draw any broad, qualitative distinctions between Tannaim who lived before the destruction and those who lived after it; they are all of one piece. The Destruction did not change them. They remained devoted to the study of the Torah and drew their spiritual life from it. *The Destruction did not weaken their spiritual life.*

As for the devastation itself, there are no similarities. Neither the Babylonians nor the Romans were racists; neither sought to destroy a whole people—man, woman, and child—because they belonged to a lower race. The Babylonians and Romans were both cruel toward their enemies and crushed those who rebelled against them with hair-raising brutality, extended as well to entire families. "The King of Babylon had Zedekiah's children slaughtered at Riblah before his eyes; the King of Babylon had all the nobles of Judah slaughtered. Then the eyes of Zedekiah were put out" (Jeremiah 39:6–7). But he appears not to have touched the common folk and the poorest of the population (*dalet ha-am*). Such conquerors were empire builders, and, when they were convinced that all danger of rebellion had past, they tended to deal mercifully with the inhabitants of their empires. A portion of Israel's population, the common folk and the poor, remained at home; another portion, the aristocrats and the intelligentsia, were forced to exchange residencies with a foreign population, on the assumption that, in their new setting, they would find it more difficult to organize new rebellions. As further evidence that Nebuchadnezzar was not a racist, we may note that he left a remnant of Judah's population behind and appointed Gedaliah son of Ahikam son of Shaphan to rule over them (Jeremiah 40:12). If Ishmael son of Nathalia had not killed Gedaliah son of Ahikam, then, despite the dislocations caused by the exile in Babylon, the fundamental institutions of Judean social life would have remained intact under Nebuchadnezzar's rule. Would Jeremiah have encouraged the Remnant of Judah to remain in the land under the protection of the King of Babylon if Nebuchadnezzar had been a second Hitler? From outside sources, we know that the exiles lived in peaceful regions of Babylon, free, under local rule. Is this what happened in our generation? In our generation, whoever revealed any sign of Jewishness was killed, whether toddler, or child, or old and infirm. How is it possible to make comparisons?

What I have said concerning the Babylonians applies also to the Romans in the initial phase of their rule. Almost two hundred years passed between the Roman conquest of the land (in the middle of the first century B.C.E.) through their suppression of the Bar Kokhba rebellion (which they ended by murdering the population). Through this period, as long as the Romans could maintain their hegemony, they did not intervene in the inner life of the occupied population—its religion and culture. They demanded signs of submission from the elders and the leaders of the population (which were expected on the birthdays of Caesar or on any special days of celebration); and, of course, they were interested in taxes and soldiers. But they left all other matters in the hands of the local inhabitants. The Jews exploited this opportunity and periodically broke out in rebellion until the Romans eventually came to despise them and to make plans for suppressing this "rebellious tribe." The suppression was ruthless. The Romans slaughtered the population, sold them into slavery, and tore down the fundamental institutions of Jewish life. Had the rebels given in, the Romans would not have crushed the Bar Kokhba rebellion with such barbarous cruelty. *One must not compare the suppression of a rebellion with the annihilation of an entire population that wants to live in peace.*

It is difficult for me for to imagine that anyone who was himself in a concentration camp—and whose own flesh bore signs of the destruction of an entire people, by way of horrible sufferings—would compare what he saw to any other event in history. There have, indeed, been other events of mass murder, but nothing that achieved the total destruction of a people. For those whose information comes only from news reports, word of mouth, and books, it may be difficult to distinguish between one tragedy and another; and the shock of what they hear or read may numb their sense of perception and lead them to suppose that all these tragedies are the same. But it is not so. *There is a hierarchy even among tragedies, and the tragedy that met our generation belongs at the top. It is unparalleled in history.*

A KABBALISTIC RESPONSE

Earlier, I rejected the notion that the Shoah is a consequence of sin, and I attributed it, instead, to human evil, which reached its terrible apogee in our days. At the same time, I also recognize that this notion is comforting to Jews who believe that God intervenes in history for the good of Israel, so long as the people's sins could not tip the scales of judgment against them. Since, in our day, the scales were certainly tipped against Israel, God did not in fact intervene. According to this reasoning, however, if the Shoah were not the result of sin, then it would be difficult to explain why God was apparently indifferent in our days and chose not to intervene. Why, for example, did God intervene with the Egyptians (bringing them plagues, against the laws of nature) or in the time of Ahasueros and Haman (in a manner consistent with nature) but not in Auschwitz? Why in Auschwitz did He lend human evil unlimited authority to destroy and be destroyed? Did God's promise to Jeremiah not obligate Him, as it were, to intervene every time Israel was in danger of annihilation and to prevent it? Why did He not prevent the worst annihilation in human history? There is no answer.

I sympathize with those who claim that in order for a person to achieve responsibility for his actions, he must first be fully free, without any obstacles and external influences. To be sure, the knowledge of good and evil itself influences a person to choose the good; but, when he chooses evil, he must, in order to merit punishment, have committed evil fully out of free choice, without any external intervention. Any kind of intervention, even from God, reduces a persons' responsibility for his actions.[17] It is possible, therefore, that God will remain aloof. In order not to diminish a persons' freedom to act—and thereby diminish his responsibility—God may stand apart, facing utter evil without intervening and without responding. Something like

this happened in the time of the Shoah. God did not intervene and
did not respond but stood apart.

The well-known homilies on the verse "I am with him [Israel] in suffering" (*imo anokhi b'tsara*: Psalms 93:16) may have been offered in this
spirit. The Holy One grieves for Israel's grief but without putting an
end to it, because He does not want to intervene in humanity's freedom to perform evil. But this homily is also applied when Israel suffers because they have sinned and God has punished them. Thus, for
example, in Midrash Lamentations, "When they sinned and their enemies entered Jerusalem, . . . the Holy One said 'I wrote in the Torah, *I
am with him in suffering*, but now that my children are overladen with
suffering, shall I remain at ease?" (chapter 2, at the end of section 6).
God grieves for the grief of Israel even when Israel causes it.

Intentionally, I have not made any use of the concept of "the hiding of God's face" (*hester panim*) that is so prevalent in the literature
of Holocaust theology.[18] According to this concept, God hid His face
during the time of the Shoah and allowed whatever happened to happen. I reject this notion, because, as indicated in Deuteronomy, the
"hiding of God's face" arises as a consequence of sin (31:17–18). This
meaning appears explicitly in Isaiah: "Your sins have made Him turn
His face away and refuse to hear you" (59:2). If we believed that "the
hiding of God's face" prevailed during the Shoah, then it would be as
if we attributed the Shoah to sin, which is the very notion that we have
rejected. God, as it were, restrained Himself from taking part in history and gave humanity an opportunity to display its capacities, for
good or for evil. It is our misfortune that, in the time of the Shoah,
humanity displayed its capacities for unprecedented evil.

But the question still persists: Why during *our* generation in particular did God choose not to intervene, despite His having intervened
in previous epochs to save Israel from annihilation? Why in *our* generation in particular did He choose not to interfere with the freedom
and moral license of evildoers, when He did interfere in previous
times and even hardened Pharaoh's heart? Why was our generation
singled out?

I certainly have no answer to this question and must be instructed
by Isaiah's words,[19] when he rebuked King Hezekiah and said, according to Talmudic tradition, "Why do you concern yourself with the
secrets of the Merciful One?" (*b'hadi kivshi d'rachmana lamah lakh?*—
Berakhot 10a). Indeed! But I still long to find an appropriate metaphor
to capture the singular fate of our generation, who suffered so terribly,

not because of anything they did or as a result of any misdeeds of their own. It was their misfortune to have lived at a time during which cosmic adjustments had to be made between the human creature, as a creature with free will, and the divinity that is immanent in all parts of creation, including the domain of moral choice. ("No place is empty of Him." Not for nothing do we call God *hamakom*, "The Place." Without Him, there is no existence.)

Lurianic Kabbalah teaches us[20] that, before the creation of humankind, God contracted Himself, as it were, in order to leave space for the creation of an autonomous creature—the human being. But God's presence in the formation of humankind caused the "Divine Contraction" (*tsimtsum*) itself to be contracted and thus limited, which meant that space for human freedom was also limited. In order to nurture human autonomy, it was therefore necessary to readjust the *tsimtsum*, to restore and strengthen it and, thereby, to expand the area in which humanity could exercise its free will. This readjustment was necessary because, as God contracts into Himself, He leaves a vacuum in His wake (*chillel rek*); and, since a vacuum is not self-maintaining, the divine must continually regenerate it. This means, however, that the divine continually reenters the vacuum, reintroducing divine being into its emptiness and thus, effectively, "gnawing away" at the vacuum itself. God's intervention in history, in particular the history of Israel, is among the most important sources of this "gnawing away." Lest the divine presence devour the *tsimtsum* altogether and vitiate free will, the Holy One periodically regenerates the *tsimtsum*: restoring it to its original source and thus enabling free will to function as before. This occurs very rarely and has no parallel in history. However, when it does occur, humanity would be brought to the summit of its moral freedom, to be exercised for good or for evil—from the point at which there is only a minimal of intervention from Above, until the divine has reequalized the normal balance between humanity's bounded freedom and the absolute freedom of God. At that point, God would have restored history to what we understand, according to the Tanakh, to be its normal place. Since God will continue to intervene in history, we should expect that it will be necessary, in the course of time, for the *tsimtsum* to be restored and adjusted once again. Let us hope that the free will that results from this restoration will be exercised for good and not as it was exercised in our generation.

Those murdered in the Shoah lived, as it were, outside of normal history. Their lives depended on how free will would be exercised by those whose freedom was fully liberated by the "renewal of *tsimtsum*" that took place in their days, returning the divine *tsimtsum* to what it was when humanity was created. Unfortunately for their victims and for us, those who exercised this free will exercised it in the most evil of ways, while their victims remained unprotected and undefended, without any intervention from Above. *They suffered and died, but for nothing they had done. The cause of their suffering was cosmic.*

PRAYER IN THE SHOAH

In rabbinic literature, it is said that the Holy One also prays. The source of this saying is in the Babylonian Talmud (*Berakhot* 7a), which reads,

> R Yochanan said in the name of Rabbi Yose: From where do we know that the Holy One Blessed be He Prays? [In the language of hyperbole and parable, it appears that the Holy One teaches prayer to Israel and commands them to pray.[21]] For it is said, "I will bring them to My holy mountain and lead them to rejoice in House of My prayer (*b'vet tefilati*)" (Isaiah 56:7). It does not say "in the house of their prayer" (*b'vet tefilatam*), but rather "in the house of My prayer" (*b'vet tefilati*). This teaches that the Holy One Blessed be He prays." [The Gemara then asks:] What does He pray? (*mai mitsalei?*) Mar Zutra son of Tuviya said in the name of Rav: [It is said[22] that the Holy One prays and says:] "May it be My will that My mercy conquer My anger and that My mercy redeem[23] My attribute [of strict judgment], and that I behave toward My children according to the attribute of mercy and judge them leniently (*lifnim mishurat hadin*).

A prayer by the Holy One is enigmatic. People pray because they desire something they do not have, something beyond their abilities to acquire. But the Holy One has everything in His hand, and if He needs to have His mercy conquer His anger, who can hold Him back? We must therefore explain (following the Rashbah in his commentary on the *Aggadot Hashas*) that this prayer is, as it were, God's request of the people Israel to make it possible for Him, the Holy One, to subdue His anger. It is a way of entreating Israel to reform their conduct enough to empower His mercy to rule over His anger, so that, if it were necessary to judge them, He would do so leniently (*lifnim mishurat hadin*). But if Israel's sins grew worse and their crimes increased beyond measure, then there would be no escape from their being judged measure for measure, punishment for sin, and who knows if they could survive it?

The commentators pointed out long ago, however, that the sages say explicitly that the Holy One prays. Although the Tanakh does not describe God's praying in any corporeal way, nevertheless, we may learn this indirectly from several verses of the Torah, of which the most prominent is this verse from Deuteronomy 5:26: "May it be [*mi yiten*, which is a term of prayer] that their hearts always move them to revere Me and follow all My commandments, so that it may go well with them and with their children forever!" At the same time, there is still a difference between such verses of Torah and the saying of the Rabbis. In the Torah, the purpose of prayer is to prevent sin, so that the people will not sin and thereby merit punishment ("to revere Me . . ."); and, as it is said, "the fear of heaven is not from heaven," which means that God cannot not rule over the fear of heaven or prevent humans from failing in it. The sages soften the Torah's lesson, however: "For there is no righteous person in the land who would do good and not sin" (Ecclesiastes 7:20). Punishment is a part of reality, and there is no generation without sinners or without their being punished for their sins. God's prayer is that the punishment would be restrained by the attribute of mercy.

I would add that, after the Shoah, this prayer of the Holy One acquires an additional feature: a petition directed to those who exercise free will, whether they are members of the people Israel (*b'nei brit*) or not. The petition is that they turn their hearts to the good, that they choose "what I desire" (Isaiah 56:4) and do not bring the world to chaos (*tohu vavohu*). There is no evil in history comparable to the evil power of those who exercised their free will to bring about the Shoah. They acquired this power as a consequence of the "renewal of tsimtsum" (*hitchadshut hatsimtsum*), a very rare, cosmic phenomenon. Despite the enigmatic character of "God's praying," there is reason to add this supplement to God's prayer as a metaphor for this enormous and ominous tragedy—*as if He Himself stood, as it were, powerless before these horrible events and expressed his grief in petitionary prayer.*

Now we may answer the question with which we opened this discussion: what prayer uniquely characterizes prayer in the concentration camps and forced labor camps? It is the prayer that asks God to eliminate the free will of the perpetrators and to take the reins of government back into His hands. A prayer like this is the prayer recited in the Rosh Hashanah Amidah, "God and God of our Ancestors, rule over all the world, in Your full glory. . . ." The sages, as is well known, introduced only one blessing—the "blessing of the day" (*birkat hayom*)—into the Sabbath and Holiday Amidah, as opposed to the twelve (and, later, the thirteen) petitionary blessings they introduced into the daily Amidah. The petitions introduce a note of sadness that accompanies a person when he asks about his own needs, and the sages did not want to introduce sadness into the days on which we are commanded "to rejoice and declare the day a delight" (*l'smoach ul'kro oneg*).[24] To be sure, the intermediate blessings (of Sabbath and Holiday) also include spiritual requests, such as "sanctify us in Your commandments" and "purify our hearts to serve you in truth," but the sages evidently assumed that, unlike material requests, spiritual requests intensify the flow of spiritual energy and elevate the joy of observing the holiday.

The intermediary blessings for Sabbath and Holidays have similar themes, except for the added theme of "Divine Sovereignty" (*malkhut*) on Rosh Hashanah, for which we have the supplemental phrase, "Rule over all the world in Your full glory." This addition is also unique since it does not constitute a direct petition for our own needs. It is, for example, unlike the Aleinu prayer—which it otherwise resembles[25]—because it lacks such immediate and tangible entreaties as "Remove abominations from the earth," or "To turn all the wicked of the earth to You," or, as in the prayer, "Sanctify us in Your commandments," that follows "Rule over the world. . . ." The prayer, "Rule over all the world, in Your full glory," is formulated wholly as a petition for God's own good, that He would rule, that He would be glorified, that He would appear. Its benefits for us would be solely indirect: *if* God would rule, then the government of the world would be conducted according to justice and law. But we do not make this request directly.

In the concentration camps and forced labor camps, this supplemental phrase acquired additional and decisive meanings. The prisoners perceived the incomprehensible evil that happened as the consequence of the Holy One's abdicating His rule, of His transferring the reins of government into the cruel hands of blood suckers, and of His own decision not to intervene against them but to grant them unlimited authority. Against them, they prayed, "Rule over all the world in Your full glory. And may every creature know that you created it, and everything that moves know that you move it. . . ." And they said, Now these villains behave like gods. Life and death is in their hands; by their will life is given, and by their will life is taken away. Remove this power from them and punish them according to their deeds, and then, "Every soul will say 'The Lord God of Israel is King and His dominion'"—the right and true One—"'rules over all.'"

EPILOGUE

I will conclude with what I myself experienced (*"didi hava uvdah"*), as narrated in my memoir, *The Book and the Sword*. I was in the forced labor camp at Wolfsberg, one of the camps of Gross-Rosen (in Lower Silesia), from May 1944 until February 1945. In the camp, we were given a day off every second Sunday, during which we could remain in the camp and, ostensibly, tend to our own needs. But, since the SS were looking for "volunteers" for work outside the camp and such "volunteering" consumed the entire day in hard labor, whoever could would hide from them. On Sundays, unlike regular days of work, the SS did not call names according to their lists but would seize people as they found them. Whoever was not caught this way was able to avoid the claws of the SS. But, when there was a shortage of workers, the SS went searching, and whoever was caught could anticipate a whipping if not more. One time I was one of those caught. I was hiding under a bed, and an SS trooper entered the room. The room was supposed to be empty, but, like a dog, he smelled the scent of flesh. When he raised his whip, I pleaded with him in German, and I began saying, "Herr Überstürmfuhrer, Merciful One (*harachamim*)." *And I escaped by the skin of my teeth.*

I cannot judge how much this supplication helped me stay alive and not collapse under the lashing. But every day I grieve for having used this holy word, "Merciful One" (*harachamim*)—which appears in the sources only in relation to the Holy One—to pray for mercy from this villain. I simply knew no other words of entreaty. I drew them from the prayer book and translated them directly into German. Perhaps, subconsciously, I thought of the SS, as it were, as God. They ruled over the camp with absolute authority; life and death—literally—remained in their hands, and I unconsciously used an expression appropriate to God.

May it be Your will that, by virtue of my having understood the correct meaning of the prayer, *melokh al kol haolom kulo bekh'vodekha*, "Rule over all the world in your full glory," that all the world comes to eradicate the condition that ruled in the forced labor camp. May it be Your will to repair the damage I have caused by substituting the profane for the holy. And may we be worthy of beholding the fulfillment of the prayer, "And His dominion rules over all."

SELECTED BIBLIOGRAPHY

On the relation between the Shoah and Divine Contraction (*tsimtsum*) in Chabad tradition, see Eliezer Schweid, "The Struggles of Orthodox Judaism with the Shoah" (Heb.) (Machanayim: Kislev, 5755), 13–18; and Hans Jonas, "The Concept of God after Auschwitz," in *Out of the Whirlwind*, ed. A. H. Friedlander (Garden City, NY: Doubleday, 1968), 465–76.

On the uniqueness of the Shoah, see Emil Fackenheim, *The Jewish Return to History: Reflections in the Age of Auschwitz and a New Jerusalem* (New York: Schocken, 1978); and Steven Katz, "The Uniqueness of the Holocaust: The Historical Dimension," in *Is the Holocaust Unique?*, ed. Allen S. Rosenbaum (Boulder, CO: Westview Press, 1978), 19–37.

On the "Hiding of the Face" (*histarta panim*), see the writings of my late friend Eliezer Berkowitz, *Faith after the Holocaust* (New York: Ktav, 1973), and *With God in Hell* (New York: Sanhedrin Press, 1979); and Norman Lamm, "The Face of God: Thoughts on the Holocaust," an address delivered to students of Yeshivah College, May 6, 1986.

Those who regard the Shoah as a consequence of sin may be divided into three groups according to what they consider to be the specific sin that led to the people's destruction:

(a) *Those for whom the sin was Zionism*. This opinion is identified primarily with the Satmar Rebbe. See *Vayoel Moshe*—the Introduction, in particular—(Heb.) (New York, 1959); and "On Redemption and Ruth 4:7" (Heb.) (New York, 1967).

(b) *Those for whom the sin was the anti-Zionism of failing to make aliyah to Israel*. See Rabbi Y. S. Taichtal, *A Happy Mother of Children* (Heb.) (Jerusalem, 5743); and Rabbi Menachem Emmanuel Chartum, "Reflections on the Shoah," *Deot* 18 (Heb.) (winter 1961): 28–37; and L. Kaplan, *Tradition*, "Rabbi Isaac Hutner's 'Daat Torah Perspective' on the Holocaust: A Critical Analysis," in vol. 18 no. 3 (Fall 1980): 235–48.

(c) *In Yeshivah circles, the more widespread opinion was that the sin was the Haskalah in general (the Jewish Enlightenment) and the way the intellectuals transformed Berlin into their Jerusalem* [even though there were more survivors among the German Jews than the Polish Jews?].They cite what was written by the Baal Meschech Chochmah (R. Meir Simcha Cohen) in his commentary on *Parashat Bechukotai* (Leviticus 26:44), "Yet even then . . . ," (Heb.), and, before him, by the Netsiv in his commentary (Heb.), *The Gate of Israel* (*Sha'ar Yisrael*). There are also some who link the Shoah to the "Footsteps of the Messiah" (*ikavta d'meshicha*). See the collection of the sayings and writings of R. Elchanan Wassserman (Heb.) (New York, 5747), 10, and the "Holy Fire" (Heb.) of the Hasidishe Rebbe of *Fiasatsna* and citations from the ultra-Orthodox newspaper articles and monographs in Rabbi Y. Steinberg, *The World of the Yeshivah and the Shoah* Part II (Heb.) (Mahanayim: Kislev, 5755), 210–13. [But the "Footsteps of the Messiah" are not limited to matters of sin. Moreover, after the more than fifty years that the messiah has not come, it is difficult to see any "Footsteps of the Messiah" in the Shoah. I also have in hand an article in Yiddish, Chaim Bakan, "Why Did the Holy One Cause War II?" (I do not know the name of the book in which the article appears). The author also cites the *Paths of Life and Peace* by Rav of Munkatz (Heb.); the *Ot Tarna*, a commentary on the introduction to the rabbinical responsa *Achiezer*, Part III (Heb.); and Steiffler, *Life of the World* (Heb.), according to which the Shoah began in Germany because of the assimilation and reform that took place among German Jews. Steiffler also cites the opinion that the Shoah came to repair the sins of all the previous generations. The souls that had previously sinned were reincarnated and made to suffer terrible trials in order to be cleansed of their sin. "This is the accounting that has gone on now for one thousand years." [And those who were killed were all from the same reincarnated souls?]

Among other approaches:

B. Maza, *With Fury Poured Out: A Torah Perspective on the Holocaust* (Hoboken, NJ: Ktav, 1986) identifies three categories of sin behind the Shoah: Zionism, assimilation, and secularism. The author writes, "We see that now decades after the Shoah, there is a renewal of Torah. . . . Perhaps it was therefore the will of the Creator to sacrifice those [who died in the Shoah—a million and a half children!] so that the Torah and the people Israel [!] would live. This citation also appears in a work by Jonathan Sacks, *The Holocaust in Jewish Ideology* (London: Valentine Mitchell, 1988), 156.

Irving Greenberg offers a very different approach in his "Cloud of Smoke, Pillar of Fire," in *Auschwitz: Beginning of a New Era?*, ed. Eva Fleischer (New York: Ktav, 1977).

For a summary of these various opinions, see Eliezer Schweid (cited above); Dan Cohn Sherbok, *Holocaust Theology* (London: Lamp Press, 1989), 15–23, 56–65; the articles in J. Sacks (cited above); and Howard Joseph, "Some Jewish Theological Reflections on the Holocaust," in *Truth and Compassion: Essays on Judaism and Religion in Memory of Rabbi Dr. Solomon Frank,* ed. Howard Joseph, Jack M. Lightstone, and Michael Oppenheimer (Waterloo, Ont.: Wilfrid Laurier University Press, 1983), 191–99.

The writings cited here deal with Holocaust theology. In our essay, we discuss prayer during the Shoah. For a discussion of prayer after the Shoah, see the essay of my childhood friend, Eliezer Wiesel, "Prayer and the Modern Person," in *Jewish Prayer: Continuity and Innovation,* ed. Gabriel Chaim Cohen (Ramat Gan: The Institute for Judaism and Contemporary Thought, 1978, 13–26.

NOTES

Translated from the Hebrew by Peter Ochs. Translation first published in *Judaism: A Quarterly Journal of Jewish Life and Thought* 199, vol. 50, no. 3 (summer 2001): 268–91. Our thanks to *Judaism* editor Murray Baumgarten for his sponsorship and editorial insight. With thanks, also, to Penina and Yossi Maciano of the University of Virginia for their help on the translation.

1. The general description of Hazan Stern, as well as the citations from his memoirs, are taken from the Yad Vashem publication of the "Introduction," *Machzor Wolfsberg,* ed. B. Guterman and N. Morgenstern (Jerusalem: Yad Vashem, 5761).

2. See Psalms 83.

3. As in the commentaries on the word *"l'khalotam,"* for example, in the commentary of R. Eliahu Mizrachi on Leviticus 26. I will comment on this when we turn to consider the rabbinic sages.

4. See Psalms 118:18: "The Lord has severely afflicted me, but has not delivered me to death"; and see the Mishnah and the Gemara in *Yoma* 85b–86a.

5. According to the scholars, Jeremiah prophesied about the Remnant of Judah around the year 568 B.C.E., a year before Nebuchadnezzar conquered Egypt, in the twenty-seventh year of his reign (as written in Ezekiel 29:17).

6. See Deuteronomy 13:3 and the debate between R. Eliezer and R. Akiva in *Tosefta Sanhedrin* 4:3.

7. See also *Seder Olam* (Ritner edition) at the end of chapter 26.

8. Jeremiah's admonition, "No pity, compassion or mercy will stop Me from destroying them," applies only to individuals.

9. We may assume that Rashi based his explanation on the ancient midrash and that he had also seen *Midrash Tehilim* on Psalms 78:38: "And He is compassionate, forgives iniquity, and does not destroy, but turns His anger away and does not awaken all His wrath." The midrash adds, "all His wrath is not awakened, but a little of it is."

10. An Amora from the land of Israel, despite the fact that our editions say "Rav" Ami, who lived in the end of the third century.

11. The source of which is in the tannaitic generation that ended at the end of the second century.

12. See the Tosafot there that begins with *v'shma minah* ("from this we may infer").

13. The first baraita is also quoted in the *Sifre Deuteronomy*, chap. 339.

14. "Unlike a *kashia*, whenever it says *tiyuvta*, the law is fully nullified" (*a tradition of the Geonim*). See the lexicon, the entry for "Refutation" (*tiyuvta*), and the *Shita Mekubetset* on *Baba Batra* 52b.

15. See Rambam's commentary on *Mishnah Sota*, chap. 3, Mishnah 3.

16. Except that he is inconsistent. By using the term "multitude," he leaves it to be understood that they are the majority, while the language of "not all the sages share this opinion" leaves us a sense that they are in a minority.

17. See *Mishneh Torah*, "Laws of Repentence," chap. 5.

18. And it already appears in Abravanel in his commentary on Joshua 7:20.

19. In *Berakhot* 10a.

20. See what is written by Chaim Vital in his introduction to the book *Etz Chayim* (Tree of Life).

21. R. Saadya Gaon, as quoted in the *Sefer Yetsira* of R. Judah of Bercelona (34–35).

22. Rav did not come to comment on the words of R. Yohanan, who is younger than him, but offered these words on his own.

23. Onkolos translates Genesis 43:30, "his compassion was stirred" as "his compassion was redeemed" (*Ets Yosef*).

24. *Birkhat Hamazon* ("Grace after Meals") is an exception because it includes petitions for our material needs (in the prayer, *r'tse v'hachalitsenu*, "O strengthen us"), yet we offer it on Sabbaths as well as weekdays. Nevertheless, the commentators have already reflected on this and accepted it.

25. Both of them may possibly have been composed by the same author. We know that the Aleinu was composed by Abba Arikha (Rav), who died in the middle of the third century in Babylonia.

2

Restoring Scripture

David Weiss Halivni

Editor's Introduction

Peter Ochs

In his prologue and epilogue, Halivni states in starkest terms the theological lesson he draws out of the Shoah: "At Auschwitz, God absented Himself from Israel, abandoned us and handed us over to the enemy." In "Prayer in the Shoah," he renarrates the lesson as a cosmic drama of *tsimtsum*: God contracts Himself to leave room for human freedom; when He sees His Presence has "leaked" back in too much, He contracts Himself again, opening a time of maximal human freedom; the Shoah corresponded to such a time. Halivni then reenacts his lesson as a religious directive: this time of God's absence is a time to pray for Him to return and rule over us again. In the present chapter, "Restoring Scripture," Halivni articulates a second part of the religious directive: to pray for divine rule is also to seek out the plain sense of God's will in the Torah. God's absence has left its mark on Jewish textual study as well as on human history. God's absence lends text scholars the freedom to read well, which means to seek out God's intention, or to misread, which means to force their own human reasoning onto the text.

Halivni's conclusion is that the health of Judaism after the Shoah requires our seeking out God's intention, but that this seeking is a matter of human will and human reason as well as of prayer. Halivni argues that, in a time of God's near-absence, even our religious leaders lack an intimate relation with the divine presence, so that even they cannot be sure that God guides their subjective interpretations of

the traditional sources. There are therefore religious as well as academic reasons to treat such interpretations with caution or even suspicion while we turn, more patiently, to the incremental work of textual science. The goal of this work is to uncover the plain sense of
every layer of Torah. At the same time, Halivni has an expansive understanding of "science," as we will now explain.

In the book's introduction, I suggest that Halivni pursues four complementary but different levels of textual scholarship: three that fall
within the sphere of the academy (plain sense, deeper plain sense, and
religious historiography or "depth historiography") and one that falls
outside it (theology). The order in which we list these levels makes a
difference. In previous writings, Halivni has presented his arguments
according to the order of his text study, addressing the plain sense first
and then introducing other dimensions of inquiry and explanation
only when and where the plain sense remains unclear. The chapters of
this book follow the reverse order, however, as does the argument of
this chapter in particular.

To read from the plain sense first is to read in a time of relative peace,
that is, a time when we have no reason to doubt our usual habits of life
and study. In such a time we trust our eyes to tell us what is happening
in the world and our ears to deliver age-old teachings about what we
ought to do in the world. In different words, we trust our ability to see
the plain sense of the world and to hear the plain sense of our text traditions. We peer behind the plain sense only when things remain unclear on the surface, and, in times of peace, we have only modest needs
to peer behind in this way. Times without peace are times when social
events are so disruptive that, in at least some spheres of life, our customary ways of acting, believing, and even seeing no longer seem trust-
worthy: what once seemed "natural" (or self-evident in its identity and
meaning) is no longer natural. These are times when the plain sense of
both life and text traditions may seem deeply confusing or unreliable.[1]
They are times when we are therefore most likely to look for guidance
far beneath the plain sense of things. *To look for such guidance is, first, to
acknowledge that what we once took to be "nature" was only the way the
world looked in light of our presuppositions—that is, our habits, assumptions,
and beliefs, all of which are imperfect and all of which can be refined. It is,
second, to try to bring these presuppositions up to the light of day so that we
may judge which of them may no longer help us make sense of this newly dis-
rupted world. It is, third, to try to revise these presuppositions so that they may
more successfully prepare us to make sense of a changed world.*

For Halivni, the Shoah represents a condition of ultimate disruption that *calls into question every level of Judaism, every Jewish habit of study, belief, and action in the world*. The result could conceivably be irreparable uncertainty about Judaism: an inhibition to act in any of the ways we associate with Jewish belief and action. In fact, I believe there is only one discovery that keeps Halivni's premise (that all is brought into question) from leading to this despairing conclusion. This is the discovery that underlying every other layer of Jewish belief is the conviction that our God has the power not only to undo all our habits of belief (all of "nature"), but also to guide us over time to build new habits of belief (to see all of nature in a new way). Halivni cannot tolerate what he calls "smoothing over" troubling texts or covering over horrible facts of history. He is prepared to trust this Jewish conviction, because it does not require "smoothing over"—it acknowledges that terrible things happen and asserts only that, over time, God may prepare us to face these things and build new worlds. I believe that *Breaking the Tablets* shows how this conviction affects each level of Halivni's rabbinic studies: guiding transformations in his theological beliefs (in "Prayer in the Shoah"), in his religious historiography (in this chapter), and in his plain-sense scholarship (in "Breaking the Tablets and Begetting the Oral Law").

In Halivni's vocabulary, disruptions in the plain sense are "maculations." He observes such maculations in each stage of rabbinic history: in the way the Talmudic sages read the Mishnah, in the way medieval sages read the Talmud, and in the subjective ways that modern *roshe yeshiva* (heads of Talmudic schools) tend to read the words of these classic sages. Halivni argues that the greatest source of error in rabbinic scholarship is the practice of *covering over* maculations in the works of previous sages. The cover-up is achieved, he says, through *forced interpretation (dochok)*: which is to employ various literary devices to show—or make it appear —that the earlier sages' works are not maculated (are not contradictory or confused or misplaced). Halivni finds forced interpretations doubly problematic because they not only misrepresent their source texts but also deflect their readers' attention away from antecedent errors in the tradition.[2] These are efforts, in other words, to cover over what seems confusing in the plain sense rather than uncovering the deeper sources of the confusion. For Halivni, *these efforts to cover over textual confusions are like efforts, in times of social disruption, to cover over our actual confusions about how to understand and act in the world. His response to the cover-up is the same in both cases. We need to face the reality of such confusions, no matter how frightening. We need to describe and identify them. We need to offer our best hypotheses about the sources (mekorot) of the confusions, and, if at all possible, we need to propose ways of resolving them. This is the work of restoration. Ideally, it is to repair maculated traditions (masorot) and presuppositions so that the original sources—the plain sense of what God says and what the world is—may shine through. Short of the ideal, it is to pursue the plain sense nonetheless, in the hope of drawing that much nearer to the truth, while we await a time of God's drawing nearer to us.*

As introduced in this chapter, there are perhaps five levels of restoration, generating five directives for Torah study after the Shoah:

(a) To promote *restoring the plain sense* as the primary goal of *all levels of Torah study, from Bible to Mishnah to Talmud.* This is to seek to uncover *torat emet*, the plain truths of what the Torah says, however difficult it will be to discern the plain truths underneath many levels of forced interpretation. For a time, specifically, of God's near absence, this is to promote the discipline of text-historical science as the *traditional as well as academic* scholar's primary means of examining the texts of Torah. Within the accepted canons of academic studies, this is to promote *plain-sense historiography*; but other levels of scientific inquiry are now urgently needed as well.

(b) To promote *deeper plain-sense historiography*, which means to deepen our sensitivity to the literary as well as historical dimensions of the plain sense.[3]

(c) To promote *depth historiography*, which means to peer beyond the plain sense when the plain sense is maculated. This means to expand the limits of historiography so that historians of the text may themselves speculate about the deeper layers of redaction and history that lie beneath our received texts. Depth historiography also includes speculations about the deeper layers of belief and presupposition that lie beneath the sages' habits of text reading. Halivni suggests that, to offer reasonable speculations at this time, historians must draw on the resources not only of other academic writings but also of communal traditions. In *Mekorot Umasorot,* for example, he often speculates about how forced interpretations could have arisen and about how they could now be replaced by cleaner readings of the *mishnaic* sources. He explains that his speculations arise out of his sense of which readings of the text would best cohere, not only with the corpus before him, but also with the unfolding practice of Torah study and with the religious needs of his community and of the broader community of Israel today.

Depth historiography provides ways of serving both community and academy without cover-up or forced reading.

(d) To recover the wisdom of classic and medieval sages who taught that deeper Torah study requires deeper preparations of the body and spirit as well as the mind. This time of crisis is an appropriate time for scholars to reconsider such study guidelines as those of Maimonides. Maimonides assumed that advanced scholarship requires preliminary exercises, not only in language, text, and history but also in logic, mathematics, natural science, and the moral and spiritual virtues, including prayer. These exercises are undertaken to open the mind and soul to perceive the patterns of relation, presupposition, and meaning that may lie under the source texts. The strictly modern academy and the anti-academic modern *yeshivot* may each remove a different set of such exercises from the curricula of scholars in training, nurturing more narrowly defined and more mutually exclusively communities of scholarship. If it were restored, the broader curriculum of exercises might help these scholarly communities reappraise their differences as complementary rather than as mutually exclusive.

(e) *To respect scientific and halakhic approaches to Talmud study as different yet complementary rather than as mutually exclusive.* This teaching refines Halivni's earlier claim that the two approaches are noncontradictory because they are mutually exclusive. In *Midrash, Mishnah, and Gemara*, he claimed that his scientific study of the Talmud is performed for its own sake and is not meant to influence religious practice. The halakhah goes according to the majority opinion of a given generation (*acharei rabim lehatot*), and he shapes his halakhic judgments in that manner. Halivni's current teaching adds a third dimension that subtly repositions the other two. He now argues that God's closeness to Israel has changed throughout history and that the method and goal of Torah study should be influenced by our sense of this distance. The relation of science to religious practice is not static but changes in response to each generation's sense of God's distance. In this chapter, Halivni argues that, in the days of the Great Assembly, God was close enough to Israel that the sages could, with divine approval, make legal judgments that went against the plain sense of Scripture. Since the time of the Talmud, however, God's distance from us has grown so great that midrashic interpretation bears the mark of human effort alone. The plain sense is the only direct trace of God's presence, and, covered over as it is by so many layers of forced interpretation, Talmudic science is our only means of recovering how the early sages may have heard the Torah.

For Halivni, therefore, science is now an instrument of *talmud torah* rather than an impediment to it. The instrument does not work directly, however. As in any science, Talmudic science offers theories rather than direct descriptions. This means that Talmudic science does not directly translate into new guidelines for legal interpretations. At the same time, Halivni now also claims that these theories are not mere intellectual exercises. They *do* bear potential implications for the *halakhah, but there is no general or scientific rule for translating scientific theory into legal guidelines.* It takes considerable time before scholarly theories about the texts of Torah achieve enough consensus that religious scholars may reconsider traditional readings in light of them—and considerably more time before religious communities would potentially link new readings to reforms in practice. Legal judgments differ, moreover, from community to community. It takes a long time, therefore, before science would have influence on practice. Even to think of such influence, however, is to introduce a third space of potential dialogue between the spheres of science and of halakhah. It is to acknowledge that each sphere may make its own contribution to *talmud torah.* If the plain sense brings one closer to God's will, then science cannot ultimately be an impediment to piety. If, on the other hand, one's halakhic practice complements the Torah reading of some generation of readers, then this practice also makes its contribution to Talmudic science: disclosing potentially unique evidence about some layer in the rabbinic chain of transmission.

NOTES

1. Wherever doubt rules over habit at such times, the result may be either inhibition (the fear of taking any action) or reflection (the impulse to think rather than act). The reflection may feed on itself (substituting a world of thought or fancy for the world of actual events), or it may begin to resemble what we call "science": an effort to account for what changed in the social environment and to propose what could be done either to reverse the change or to adapt our actions to it. To offer such proposals is, first, to acknowledge that what we once took to be "nature" was only the way the world looked in light of our habits, assumptions, and beliefs, all of which are imperfect and all of which can be refined. It is, second, to take responsibility for our worldviews as well as our actions. To respond reflectively to social disruption is to reframe our actions and our view of the world as subject to at least some choice.

2. For Halivni, forced interpretations impede the efforts of future scholars to discover maculations in the text traditions and, by repairing them, to help restore the sources of Torah.

3. For a parallel approach, see Steven Fraade, *From Tradition to Commentary: Torah and Its Interpretation in the Midrash Sifre to Deuteronomy* (Albany: State University of New York Press, 1991), 13–14.

Restoring Scripture

We long for the unadulterated word of God.

PREFACE

In personal conversations I have often used the term *tikkun hamikra* or "repairing Scripture" to describe the task of those who have accepted some of the conclusions reached by methods of historical criticism as applied to the study of Bible and Talmud. These scholars are cognizant of inconsistencies, repetitions, and irregularities within the text of Sacred Scripture. And yet, while accepting the critical approach to Scripture, they still believe in *Torat Moshe:* the revelation of both the Written and Oral Laws at Mount Sinai. They attribute the corruption of the text to human error, a consequence of the "Sins of Israel," *chate'u yisrael* (a phrase I adapt from the Babylonian Talmud, *Sanhedrin* 21a). According to the Talmudic teaching, the Sins of Israel began with the Golden Calf (forty days after the Torah was received at Sinai) and continued until Ezra's time (when the children of Israel returned to monotheism and Mosaic Law). There was then an ongoing process of "maculation" of the scriptures, which resulted in textual inconsistencies and linguistic irregularities. As it is well known, there was a time (apparently during the period of the reigns of Manasseh and Josiah, kings of Judah) during which the Mosaic Law was forgotten and the children of Israel practiced idolatry. It was at this time that the original text was neglected, allowing inconsistent and conflicting sources, as well as other flaws, to permeate the original text. After the lost Scripture was found (during the reign of Josiah, close to the time of the destruction of the First Temple) and even after Ezra and his entourage restored the ancient tradition, some traces of these corruptions were not eradicated, thus leaving the text flawed in various places.

With the neglect of the Written Torah, the Oral Torah was forgotten as well, for indeed, without the Written Law there cannot be any Oral Law. Unlike the Written Torah, the Oral Torah was not discovered during the reign of Josiah, and it consequently lacked original documentation until the arrival of the early rabbinic sages (*Tannaim*). Continuing a restoration that began in Ezra's time, these sages restored the Oral Law by means of the Midrashic method, rereading the received text according to the exegetical principles by which the Torah is expounded. As introduced in Ezra 7:10—"And Ezra had set his heart to seek (*l'drosh*) the Law of the Lord"—*l'drosh* means to engage in exegetical interpretation, and this is the first time that we find the combination of words *derash* and Torah. Previously, *l'drosh* had only the more general meaning of "ferreting out" or "seeking: as when Rebecca's two children "struggled in her womb. . . . And she went to inquire (*l'drosh*) of the Lord" (Genesis 25:22). In Ezra and Nehemiah, *l'drosh* acquires the additional meaning of textual exegesis. By the end of the Talmudic period, when faith in the validity of this Midrashic method was undermined, the later generations of rabbinic sages, or *Amoraim*, validated some practices by resorting to the general declaration that some laws were given to Moses at Sinai (*halakhah lemoshe misinai*). Reducing explanation to mere declaration, the Amoraim no longer lived up to the higher standards of textual exegesis.

In these terms, the task of a religious person—one who believes in the Sinaitic revelation—is to restore the maculated text, the text that was corrupted through the "Sins of Israel." The believing Jew must restore the Written and Oral Torah to their original state. It is within this context that I have used the expression *tikkun hamikra* to describe this process of restoring the Sacred Scriptures. *Tikkun hamikra* is a critical attempt to bring the Scriptures closer, as close as possible, to their original form as revealed to Moses at Mount Sinai.

PRIOR USES OF THE TERM "TIKKUN HAMIKRA"

I have adopted the expression *tikkun hamikra* from the *Sifra Parashat Shemini*, 4:5, the only place where the expression can be found in rabbinic literature. The meaning of the expression remains ambiguous. To begin with, the Hebrew root *tkn* bears a broad range of meanings, including "to prepare," "to enhance," "to repair something broken": for example, "To make straight (*l'taken*) that which he has made crooked" (Ecclesiastes 7:13); "They said to R. Akiva, one does not tell a person to pervert his ways in order that he could then correct (*yitaken*) them" (*Tosefta Hallah*, 1:9). When the words *tikkun* and *mikra* are combined, the range of possible meanings is even greater, as reflected in the commentators' divergent readings of this expression in the *Sifra*. While we cannot, therefore, specify the exact meaning of this expression in the *Sifra*, we can be reasonably certain that the expression concerned an effort to enhance or improve a given text.[1] My use of the term *tikkun hamikra* is therefore unlike that of the *Sifra*. I use the concept of *tikkun* in its by now well-known kabbalistic sense, as conveyed in the Lurianic notion of *olam hatikkun*, "mending the world." According to Isaac Luria, the world has been broken—through a process he calls "the breaking of the vessels"—and it now needs to be mended. This, I believe, is akin to Israel's sinful neglect and thus maculation of the sacred texts of Torah—"the breaking of the tablets"—which now need to be mended.

As previously mentioned, the traditional commentators on the *Sifra* did not agree on the meaning of the unique term, *tikkun hamikra*. The Rabad offers two solutions[2]: *tikkun hamikra* means (1) "that we should be knowledgeable concerning the animals and their names" and (2) "it is more pleasant and fitting that the text state a clean sign before an unclean sign." According to the first explanation, *tikkun hamikra* concerns the reader's edification; according to the second, it concerns the enhancement of the text. The author of the *Korban Aharon* states, "The verse should not begin with an unclean sign."[3] The Malbim understands the term as referring to the customary style of Scripture, which is to repeat itself: "This is the way of the biblical text—that each verse refers only to itself [rather than a general case]."[4] In contrast, the Vilna Gaon considered the term unnecessary and erased it completely from the text.[5]

What, then, was the original intent of the *Sifra*, and which one of the exegetes has understood the expression correctly? It seems to me that the answer lies in the very question that the *Sifra* asks concerning the manner of listing of the unclean animals found in Leviticus 11:4–6:

> Nevertheless, these shall you not eat of them that chew the cud, or of them that divide the hoof: the camel, because he chews the cud but does not part the hoof, he is unclean to you. And the rock badger, because he chews the cud but does not part the hoof, he is unclean to you. And the hare, because he chews the cud but does not part the hoof, he is unclean to you.

Concerning these verses, the *Sifra* asks,

> What do these verses come to teach us? If it is for *tikkun hamikra*, behold it is written elsewhere [in shorter form] — ". . . the camel, the hare, and the rock badger for they chew the cud, [but do not divide the hoof, therefore they are unclean to you]" (Dt. 14:7). So what have these verses come to include?

If we can point to just what the *Sifra* found to be problematic about the three verses in Leviticus, then perhaps we could understand the sages' intended definition of *tikkun hamikra*.

The *Sifra* is certainly puzzled by the repetitive nature of the three verses. We could conceivably explain this redundancy in several possible ways: (1) Perhaps verses 4 to 8 are not necessary at all because we are already informed in verse 3 that it is permitted to eat only animals that possess two signs: that they chew their cud and have split hooves. This is certainly the style of the text a bit further on (verses 9 to 10) where the signs for permissible fish—fins and scales—are the subject under discussion; (2) Or perhaps the camel, rock badger, and hare, who all possess only one of the two signs, could have been economically included in one verse, as they are in Deuteronomy 14; (3) Or perhaps only the phrase "they chew their cud" was objectionable to the *Sifra* because these are, after all, unclean animals even though they do possess one clean sign.

The second of these understandings seems strongest since the *Sifra* mentions only the camel, rock badger, and hare and fails to include in its question the similar case of the pig (which is discussed later on). As the *Sifra* itself points out, Deuteronomy 14 shows that all of these animals could have been included in one verse. Therefore, the Malbim's understanding of the phrase *tikkun hamikra* as stylistic seems to be the most appropriate: "that each verse refers only to itself" rather than including all the cases within itself. Thus, the *Sifra* counters such an argument by bringing a verse from Deuteronomy to demonstrate that Scripture can—and in fact here does—employ language in a generalizing way, referring to a whole set of items rather than just one particular. As for the other exegetes, both the Rabad (according to his second explanation) and the author of the *Korban Aharon* understand the problem in terms of our third possibility: that the redundancy of the phrase "they chew their cud" is apparently what perplexed the *Sifra*. Accordingly, the expression *tikkun hamikra* means "to enhance the text." In other words, it is more appropriate and fitting that Scripture mentions a clean sign before an unclean and disqualifying sign, as it also does when it mentions the clean and then the unclean signs of the pig. Lastly, Rabad, according to his first explanation, perceived that any mention of a camel, hare, or rock badger is redundant (since the signs for clean animals were already given in verse 3, we would know that these animals were unclean). He therefore argued that the meaning of *tikkun hamikra* was to enhance *our* knowledge of the world: "that we should be knowledgeable concerning the [physical characteristics of the] animals and their names."

In any event, none of the traditional explanations of this unique expression, *tikkun hamikra*, concern correcting a defective text. I am therefore using the term in a nontraditional way, combining the words *tikkun* and *mikra* without regard to the way they have previously been combined.

It is also important to note that my use of the expression *tikkun hamikra* differs from that of the sages of the *Sifra* in another respect. The sages were not referring to the entire biblical text. According to their use of the expression, the Torah is not in need of a general *tikkun*; just those three verses in Leviticus were under scrutiny, for they seemed redundant. The *Sifra* therefore appears to have coined the expression to account for the apparent repetition of a few verses found in Leviticus. In contrast, I apply the expression *tikkun hamikra* to the entire Torah because I consider the need for *tikkun* to be pervasive. I contend that the Written Torah was "maculated" through a process of forgetfulness and neglect that I call *chate'u yisrael* and that it is therefore in need of a general restoration in order to "reinstate its glory as in the days of old." Here too I am closer to the kabbalistic rendering of the concept of *tikkun*. According to the Lurianic theory, *tikkun olam* refers to the need for repairing a defect in the process of creation itself, not just an adjustment here and there of certain flawed details.

As employed frequently throughout the *tannaitic* literature, the phrase *tikkun ha-olam* has a meaning similar to that of the *Sifra* and unlike that conveyed by the Lurianic teaching. In the *tannaitic* literature, *tikkun* is used in the sense of prevention, to eliminate obstacles that could cause damage to the community, both material and spiritual damage. The case of material damage is illustrated in *Mishnah Gittin* 4:3: "Hillel instituted the *prosbul* because of *tikkun ha-olam*."[6] The case of spiritual damage is illustrated by the Mishnah's use of the similar expression *tikkun hamizbeach*; "So that the altar will not be desolate and the priests melancholic and this would prevent them from doing the sacrificial service" (*Gittin* 55a). In sum, as used in the Mishnah, the expression *tikkun ha-olam* does not mean to mend the world or to suggest that there is a flaw in creation. Instead, the term *tikkun* refers to the necessity of adjusting certain legal situations that can, intentionally or unintentionally, be injurious to society. The term *olam* here refers to the proper running of society as a whole.

Why, then, was this expression used only once in the *Sifra*? I conclude that the expression was avoided not because it refers to only a few verses in Scripture but because *tikkun* also bore the more prevalent connotation of "repairing that which is damaged," and the *Sifra* deemed this an unacceptable use of language in relation to the Sacred Scriptures. I believe it was for the same reason that the term *tikkun ha-olam* is not to be found outside the Mishnah and Tosefta (except for the instances in which it has been borrowed from elsewhere[7]). As previously mentioned, the verb *tkn* was sometimes taken in the sense of "to improve": "And here we have made a great improvement" (*Mishnah Succah* 5:2). The Aleinu prayer, thought to be of mid-third-century provenance, the same period of Rav's literary activity, calls for the rule of God: "To repair (*tkn*) the world by establishing the kingdom of *Shaddai*." This is not to be understood, however, in the sense of fixing a world that has gone awry, for the kingdom of God on earth was never in fact actually established. Rather, this is a prayer for the future, a call "to enhance the world by establishing (sometime in the future) the kingdom of *Shaddai*."

After the Talmudic period there was a shift in the meaning of the verb *tkn*. The prevalent sense was now "to repair that which was already damaged," as in our usage. This stands in contradistinction to the former *tannaitic* usage, which was to prevent a future legal difficulty and the social ills that would most likely ensue. As it was received by the Amoraim, the expression *tikkun olam* thus carried an ambiguous set of meanings and could not be used with any certainty. Perhaps for this reason, the expression fell out of use until it was revived out of dormancy by Isaac Luria at a much later date in a period when the world was perceived to be in need of cosmic repair.

My use of the expression *tikkun hamikra* is most similar to the Lurianic notion of repairing what was broken in the beginning. In my reading, Scripture needs restoration because its text has suffered maculation since its inception. The process of maculation began with the sin of the Golden Calf, a mere forty days after the Torah was given at Sinai. As the sages lament, "If only the first Tablets had not been broken, then Israel would not have forgotten the Torah" (*'Eruvin* 54a). The maculation of the biblical text continued for approximately 700 years until it was corrected by Ezra the Scribe. Unfortunately, even he could not eradicate all of the defects embedded in the text, and so they remain. It is incumbent on each and every generation to investigate the Torah anew, to explain its difficulties and to correct them. When God gave Israel the Torah, it was with the foresight that in only forty days they would worship a golden calf, continue to worship idols for many centuries to come, and thus be incapable of observing its precepts. Their inability to fulfill the Torah did not prevent the Almighty from giving it to them. He did not force them to accept it under duress but wanted them to bear both the Yoke of Heaven and the Yoke of the Law of their own accord, by choice and free will, as related in the Torah itself. Eventually they did choose to take it on themselves, but in the meantime the text underwent a process of maculation. It remains our obligation to engage actively in the ongoing project of restoring this maculated text, investigating its defects, and making every effort to discover anew the words of the Living God as they were originally revealed at Sinai.

THE NEED TO REPAIR FORCED INTERPRETATIONS

If the text of the Written Torah, Scripture, is marred by maculation, the text of the Talmud is marred by forced interpretation, *dochok:* the effort to cover over, or rationalize, the maculations of received texts rather than seeking to repair or at least acknowledge them. This defect of the Talmud inhibits our capacity to study *torat emet*, the Torah as it was given. First of all, the forced interpretations introduce a kind of reasoning that is foreign to the texts they seek to explain. Second, by covering over defects in the received texts, these interpretations prevent us from seeing those defects and, thereby, from taking on, let alone fulfilling, the obligatory work of repairing them. Since we belong, still, to the generations of those whose life in Torah is defined by how we read Talmud, the Talmud's forced interpretations remain an obstacle to our living lives of Torah. I therefore extend the obligation of *tikkun hamikra* to the work of restoring the original texts of the *Tannaim*, the authors of the Mishnah, and restoring the correct reasonings of the *Amoraim*, the authors of the *Gemara*. This has been my lifelong work in *Mekorot Umasorot*. In this closing section, I seek to explain how the work of repairing forced interpretations contributes to the overall work of *tikkun hamikra*.

There were commentators who, after noticing that the Talmud sometimes will give a nonliteral, forced interpretation, thought that this was entirely plausible and even correct.[8] For example, the Hatam Sofer wrote, "The majority of the forced interpretations are true, whereas most of the rational ones or 'discovered' ones are false—and they mask the truth."[9] Less extreme is the formulation of R. Israel Salanter: "'What is the truth'? The truth does not reside only within the literal meaning, for that is but only one of the categories of evidence used in textual interpretation, and in the majority of cases concerning difficult questions of interpretation . . . the non-literal interpretations militate against the literal ones and push them aside, as we see from the Talmud when the sages limit the application of the text to a situation not mentioned at all in that text (an *okimta*)."[10] Once, I heard from a certain rabbi that the adage "The text does not stray from its literal meaning" (*Shabbat* 63a) pertains only to the biblical text but that the Mishnah (and the Talmud) are to be understood nonliterally. Proof of this position is garnered from the fact that sometimes the Talmud is forced to claim that the Mishnah must have omitted a phrase (*chasurei mechsera*). These commentators viewed the forced interpretations of the Talmud as preferable, as explanations of choice rather than of necessity. In contrast, compare the Talmud's statement in *Ketubot* 42b: "But a forced interpretation is not how we interpret."[11] It is interesting to note that these commentators prefer a smooth and simple interpretation over a forced one and use forced interpretations only when they have no recourse. Even so, theoretically, they are willing to grant that a forced interpretation has its advantages over a literal one (*kepeshuto*) because of the prevalence of these cases in the literature. This covering over of difficult meanings is what I consider the "flaw" in the Rabbis' reception of Torah; its repair is what I call "Restoring Scripture."[12]

Actually, the proliferation of forced interpretations has its basis in one of two situations: either because many texts are indeed corrupt or because we ourselves possess unnecessary assumptions and thus force texts to accommodate our own preconceived notions. A corrupt text is one that suffers from either missing or extra words or letters, and we must correct the text in order to understand it properly. Now, sometimes we can be right on target and we can correct it, but, more often, the commentators evade the issue of corruptions and therefore force a far-fetched interpretation on the text.

I will illustrate this with a lesser-known presumption I have called the "unity of the sources" (*echud hamekorot*). This is the assumption that each and every sage knew everything that his opponent knew, and, therefore, if one sage did not accept the other's view, we are obligated to find the issue or argument that could warrant such a disagreement. We would be hard pressed to locate such an issue or argument, and, in order to validate our assumption, we might have to force an inappropriate interpretation on the text. Assuming the "unity of the sources," furthermore, this issue or argument would have to be such that the opponent could counter it with satisfactory explanations of his own, and this affords even more opportunity for forced interpretation of the text. Occasionally, the Talmud will ask, "And how holds the other one?" (how does the other sage counter the argument of his opponent?), or "R. so and so, what reason did he have not to hold like R. so and so [his opponent]"? These instances are few, however, and, in our opinion, later additions. It would seem that, at an earlier stage of compilation, the Talmud recognized that opponents in an argument need not know each others' reasons, so that there would no need for the Talmud to try to locate and compare these reasons. Nonetheless, the later generations attributed to their predecessors a certain unity of thought, assuming that each one was cognizant of the others' theories and rationales, and therefore, if in spite of their parity they did not agree on a particular issue, then it could only be due to a flaw in one of their positions—and they were forced to find it. Similarly, most of the medieval exegetes assumed that the Talmud could not contradict itself, not even between the different Tractates, and consequently they resorted to very forced interpretations.[13] Perhaps they thought, as did R. Shrira Gaon before them, that since on their view R. Ashi and Ravina edited the entire Talmud, they would have not left in it any contradictions, except in places that they call "interchangeable matters."[14] In the eleventh and twelfth centuries there was a movement, represented by the Rashbam and R. Joseph Bekhor Shor and others, whose intent was to interpret Scripture only according to its literal meaning, even when that meaning would conflict with the halakhah. This movement did not gain wide acceptance, and just about every commentary composed since (except those that were composed by academics) was homiletic in style.

In spite of how common they are, nonliteral interpretations are forced upon the text and strain it. We long for the unadulterated word of God, convinced as we are that forced interpretations pervert the text and His words. A forced interpretation strays from the real intent of the words and attributes to the text things it does not say, thereby transgressing both the commandments of "do not add" and "do not subtract" (to the word of God). It is preferable to leave a difficult issue unresolved rather than to force the words to say something they do not mean. If we have done so in the past, we must now resolve never to do this again in the future. We must admit our wrongdoings and confess before Him, "We have sinned by distorting Scripture" and "May we repent of this sin and thereby bring about our own *tikkun* as well."

A homily. We will end with a short, nonliteral interpretation of the well-known Mishnah found at the beginning of Tractate *Avot* (*Ethics of the Fathers*):

"Moses received the Torah at Sinai": To understand it as it was given to him, "through a clear lens," without the need to add concepts of his own.

"And he gave it over to Joshua": Joshua did not "receive" the Torah from Moses, for it was "given over" to him, to understand and to interpret according to his own conceptual abilities, "through an unclear lens."

In the distinction between receiving and being given, between the word of God and the Torah of man, a defect emerges that can be corrected only by a process of restoring Scripture. The maculation of Scripture began in the days of Joshua and not of Moses. The sages taught, "During the mourning period for Moses, minor and major laws, analogies for deriving the law and scribal exactitudes were forgotten"[15]: only then and not before.

It is our prayer that by restoring Scripture we can return to that which once was, to the state of Moses hearing the words of God, to a receiving rather than just a giving over.

NOTES

Translated from the Hebrew by Dr. Iris Felix.

1. On first glance, R. Hillel's commentary on the *Sifra*, in the Oxford manuscript, appears to offer a different reading: "in other words, to correct the biblical text." According to R. Hillel's further explanation, however, it appears that he did not, in fact, accept the notion of a defective biblical text. Neither he nor our sages entertained the possibility that the Torah was flawed.

2. RaBaD is the acronym for Rabbi Abraham ben David of Posquieres, who lived in Provence at the end of the twelfth century. All these commentaries appear in the standard editions of the Sifra.

3. *Korban Aharon* is the commentary on the *Sifra* by R. Aharon ben Avraham ibn Chayim of Morocco (1545–1632).

4. Malbim is the acronym for Rabbi Meir Leibush ben Yechiel Michel (1809–1879), biblical commentator from Volhynia, later Warsaw.

5. The Vilna Gaon was the great Torah and Talmud scholar Rabbi Eliyahu of Vilna (1720–1797).

6. The *prosbul* was a legal formula through the use of which a creditor could still claim his debts after the Sabbatical Year, despite the biblical injunction against doing so in Deuteronomy 15: 2. (See *Encyclopaedia Judaica*, 13:1181; see also *Mishnah Sheviit* 10:3.)

7. Thus, *Sifre* Deuteronomy para. 113 discusses the *prosbul* as *tikkun ha-olam* as taken from *Mishnah Gittin* 4:3; *Sifre* Deuteronomy para. 213 discusses the term *tikkun havelad* as found in *Tosefta Yevamot* 6:8; this is also true for its appearance in *Mekhilta Mishpatim* 20, "The sages restricted [it] for the sake of *tikkun ha'olam*."

8. I have already called these commentators to the readers' attention in the introduction to my book *Mekorot Umasorot* (*Sources and Traditions*), Tractate *Nashim*, 10n9.

9. See the Hatam Sofer's book of novellae on Tractate *Ketubot* (*Shayarai Teshuvot Hatam Sofer*, Satmar 5668/1908, 46).

10. In R. Israel Salanter's introduction to the journal he founded, *Tevunah No. 1* (1860).

11. See also *Temura* 21a (at the beginning of the page).

12. See also Ta-Shma, Israel H., "Bible Criticism in Early Medieval Franco-Germany," (Heb.) in, ed. Sara Japhet, *The Bible in the Light of Its Interpreters* (Jerusalem: Magnes Press, 1994).

13. See, for instance, *Tosofot Menahot* 58b *ad loc.*

14. These commentators interpreted the Talmudic verse "R. Ashi and Ravina terminated the instruction" (*Baba Metsi'a* 86a, at the beginning of the page) to mean that R. Ashi and Ravina edited the Talmud in its entirety. Modern scholars, however, interpret the word "instruction" in another manner.

15. *Temurah* 16a.

3

Breaking the Tablets and Begetting the Oral Law

David Weiss Halivni

Editor's Introduction

Peter Ochs

Halivni's voluminous commentary on the Talmud, *Mekorot Umasorot,* redresses what he considers the most conspicuous defects of the Talmud. Among the most significant of these are *dochok,* or "forced interpretation" and misapplications of the doctrine of *halakhah le moshe mi sinai*: that the Rabbis' oral law is "law given to Moses on Sinai." One of the primary contributions of the present volume is to display the theology that underlies much of the work of *Mekorot Umasorot.* "Restoring Scripture" offers a theological reason for Halivni's critique of "forced interpretation," and the present chapter, "Breaking the Tablets and Begetting the Oral Law," shows how the theology of "Restoring Scripture" applies, as well, to Halivni's critique of efforts to claim Sinaitic status for humanly constructed oral law. Halivni seeks to show, in case after case, how the later Amoraic and medieval notion of a separate oral law contradicts the evidence of Scripture and of the *tannaitic* literatures. When read in the context of this book, the essay also illustrates how this medieval notion contradicts Halivni's theological account of God's increasing distance from the authors of oral law. Modifying his own earlier claims, these two essays show how Halivni's theological response to the Shoah has in fact shaped—or at the very least closely complemented—his Talmudic science.

For Halivni, the Shoah has shown this to be a time of God's maximal distance from us. The arguments of "Restoring Scripture" imply that, at such a time, we discern God's will only through the instruments of plain-sense science and of prayer—and, even then, our discernments are probable at best. At such a time, midrash is a strictly human affair. It is an appropriate means of meeting some of our immediate needs but only if we acknowledge its strictly human provenance. Whether they are liberal or ultra-Orthodox, political or apolitical, our leaders speak only as finite human beings whose words belong to some specific time and place and set of assumptions. As for scientists, God's distance implies that they, too, lack any certain or infallible access to the truth, that is, to the divine law and will as it is displayed in the created world or in the revealed texts. They do, however, have access to creaturely tools of knowledge that enable them to make testable claims about the effects of creaturely behavior. (Testable claims are claims that are always subject to error and whose errors will be exposed through various experiments and probings or, at least, through the long run of history.) Unless God is close to them, rabbinic scholars—scientific or traditionalist—behave like other human creatures. For Halivni, the sages from Ezra's time through the time of the Tannaim enjoyed unusual closeness to God, which means that their work serves, collectively, as a reliable sign of God's will, albeit subject to complex traditions of reading. One part of their work is to have completed and sealed the canonized Written Torah. Another part is to have articulated the Oral Law that accompanies and clarifies that Torah. Halivni adds, however, that our reception of this Torah remains fallible since Ezra and the sages did not correct all the ill effects of the "Sins of Israel" (*chate'u yisrael*) and since the work of the Tannaim is itself obscured by the creaturely maculations of the Amoraim.

"Breaking the Tablets and Begetting the Oral Law" shows how Halivni's theological commitment to "Restoring Scripture" stimulates his plain-sense critique of the doctrine of *halakhah le moshe mi sinai*.

SCIENCE AND THEOLOGY IN HALIVNI'S PLAIN-SENSE SCHOLARSHIP

In a word, the primary goal of Halivni's lifelong study of the Talmud has been to recover the plain sense of the Mishnah. In his reading, the Mishnah displays the *tannaitic* sages' understanding of the plain sense of the legal dimensions of Torah and thus of the legal dimensions of

God's word on Sinai, *torat emet*. According to tradition, as it was articulated by Rav Sherira Gaon, the Talmud displays both the apodictic
rulings (or "Conclusions," *gemara*) of the Amoraim and the active discourse (or "give-and-take," *masah umatan*, in Hebrew; *shakla v'taria*, in
Aramaic) that accompanied these rulings. According to *Mekorot Umasorot*,[1] however, the Amoraim transmitted only their apodictic rulings,
with little of the accompanying discourse. Halivni's thesis is that the
Gemara that we receive in our editions of the Babylonian Talmud is a
product of much more than the Amoraim. If it were printed as the
Amoraim produced it, the *Gemara* would look more like the Mishnah:
a collection of discrete legal statements, without the lengthy debates
or give-and-take that we associate with the Talmud. Whence the Talmud, therefore? The bold claim of *Mekorot Umasorot* is that almost all
the give-and-take we read in our Talmud is the work of the anony-
mous redactors, the *Stammaim* as Halivni named them, who received
the legal judgments of the Amoraim and collected, edited, and renar-
rated them into the remarkable literature we know as Talmud. Work-
ing, in Halivni's latest estimation, from the mid-sixth to the mid-
eighth centuries, the Stammaim completed and "sealed" the *Gemara*
and thus the Talmud (or Mishnah + *Gemara*) as it was received by the
great Gaonic scholars of the ninth century. (In the introduction to his
latest Talmudic commentary, Halivni surmises that the Stammaim
were, in fact, the early Gaonim and the *Saboraim* were the last generation of *stammaitic* scholars rather than the distinct group of interpreters that scholars have traditionally portrayed them to be. He suggests that the Saboraim worked during only the last thirty to fifty years
of the *stammaitic* period, receiving from their teachers a virtually complete *Gemara* and adding only peripheral revisions and editorial comments.[2] The later Gaonim were the first to comment extensively on
the legal implications of the *Gemara* as a completed work.

In Halivni's reconstruction, the greatest contribution of the Stammaim was not only to redact three centuries of Amoraic work but also
to renarrate this work within the kind of dialogic give-and-take that
the Amoraim attribute to the *tannaitic* period. The Stammaim, in
other words, reconstructed a dramatic, oral-like environment for Jewish study of the halakhah, out of received traditions about what went
on in the *tannaitic* and amoraic study houses, out of what the
Amoraim seem to attribute to their teachers, and out of their own
imaginative and interpretive sense of the voice of Torah as religious
teaching and law.

Halivni's next major thesis has been that, in the process of editing the amoraic statements and reposing them as *tannaitic*-like legal debates, the Stammaim also committed some errors of interpretation. He focuses, in particular, on errors of "forced interpretation," *dochok*. This is their tendency to assume that the amoraic statements they received could not have been blemished by internal self-contradiction or, for example, by errant transpositions of one verse or text or author for another. When a given set of statements might seem (to our eyes) to display such blemishes, the Stammaitic tendency was to force some reading of the amoraic statements that would explain the apparent errors away, smooth them over, in Halivni's terms. One of the primary goals of *Mekorot Umasorot* is to identify instances of such forced interpretation and then speculate about what may have caused them and how they could be remedied. Halivni argues that forced interpretations appear in our version of the *Gemara* when the Stammaim wrongly assume that an Amora is commenting on the same version of Mishnah that they have before them. Halivni speculates that, in such cases, the Amora's comment must appear confused, because it does not in fact follow from the version of Mishnah that the Stammaim are considering. Covering over what we might consider a discrepancy between amoraic statement and Mishnah, the Stammaim add words that "force" the one to fit the other. Halivni's characteristic remedy is to speculate about which version sat before an Amora and which before a Stam and then to transpose the amoraic commentary back to its appropriate Mishnah. In some cases, subsequent research has uncovered just the versions that Halivni expected to see; sometimes it has not.

According to this pattern, Halivni has sought to reconstruct the primary and subsequent interpretive layers (the sources, *mekorot* and traditions, *masorot*) of tractate after tractate of the Babylonian Talmud. The overarching goal is to uncover the "true" or plain-sense character of each layer of interpretation and thus, by inference and hypothesis, of the sources underlying all these layers. Halivni characterizes his goal in plain-sense terms: to offer plausible—and, when possible, verifiable—reconstructions of as many rabbinic sources as he can. He argues that this kind of Talmudic science should prove as successful as the kind of natural science that has generated testable accounts of gravity and relativity and quantum mechanics. In neither case are we dealing with apodictic and infallible claims. Halivni assumes that both kinds of science are undertaken by fallible human beings and that both are subject to revision on the basis of new evidence and newly discovered ways of gathering evidence. Like the natural science of Einstein and Heisenberg, moreover, Halivni's Talmudic science draws on the resources of intuition and imagination as well as of observation and analysis. Halivni therefore speaks, at times, of the "music" of the rabbinic literature, the interwoven patterns of reading and interpretation that arise, for him, out of the way the many verses and layers of rabbinic Torah converse with each other or sing to each other. These intuitions ground Halivni's hypotheses about the various layers of the redacted Talmud and, in that sense, contribute directly to his academic science of the plain sense.

At the same time, Halivni's science is directly linked to his theological commitments. The massive energy he puts into *Mekorot Umasorot* is not offered for the sake of academic scholarship alone. Halivni offers his Talmudic science at what he believes is a time of crisis in Israel's relation to God. At such a time, the work of repairing textual "blemishes" in the Talmud is also a means of clearing a path to Israel's greater discernment of God's will. Forced interpretations obscure rather than clarify the arguments of the Rabbis and, thus, what they have to say about God's will. Misrepresentations of rabbinic law as *halakhah le moshe misinai* conceal rather than disclose the sources and character of post-Talmudic jurisprudence.

For Halivni, plain sense science and theology are, thus, complementary dimensions of Talmudic study. I read the great energy of his endeavor as a mark of his theological passion: to repair the text as means of helping re-open Israel's access to God's will. And I read his passion for plain-sense science as a mark of his commitment to theological repair. This is his conviction that, in a time of God's greater distance, rabbinic scholars and leaders need to acknowledge the greater influence of human judgment in their readings of Torah and the need for greater discipline in the ways they formulate, validate, and test such judgments.[3]

NOTES

1. And as summarized in Halivni's most recent introduction to all his introductions to this commentary: David Weiss Halivni, *Iyunim Behithavot Hatalmud* ("Relfections on the Formation of the Talmud")(Jerusalem: Magnes Press, 2008).

2. Halivni, *Reflections*.

3. In Steven Fraade's terms, Halivni's work displays a "double-dialogue," which means "that the commentary simultaneously faces and engages the

text that it interprets and the society of 'readers' for whom and with whom it interprets." In these terms, Halivni's work resembles what Fraade considers the method of the ancient scriptural commentaries:

> Ancient scriptural commentaries—even as they closely scrutinize the particles of the text to which they attend, are always about the texts as a *whole*. By this I mean that they not only seek for the text to be held in high regard by its interpretive community, but for the interpretive community to regard *itself* in relation to that text as mediated by its commentary. In other words, such a commentary is not simply a series of declarative assertions about the meaning of words in a text but an attempt to *effect* a relationship between that text overall and those for whom it is "scripture," predicated on the assumption not only that the text needs and deserves to be interpreted, but that the community for whom it needs to be interpreted itself needs to be engaged in the activity of interpretation to understand itself and *transform* itself into what it ought to be. Ancient scriptural commentaries are not simply constative conduits of meaning . . . but also performative media by which the polymorphic "world" of the text and that of its students are transformatively brought toward each other, while never fully merged, so as to confront each other through the double-dialogue of the commentary. By *double-dialogue* I mean that the commentary simultaneously faces and engages the text that it interprets and the society of "readers" for whom and with whom it interprets. Cited in Steven Fraade, *From Tradition to Commentary, Torah and Its Interpretation in the Midrash Sifre to Deuteronomy* (Albany: State University of New York Press, 1991), 13–14.

Breaking the Tablets and Begetting the Oral Law[*]

INTRODUCTION

The concept of a dual Torah is a commonplace in Jewish thought and in scholarship on Judaism. It is nearly universally believed that, from its earliest stages, the rabbinic tradition has conceived of two Torahs (*torot*): the Scriptures on the one hand (*torah she bekhtav*) and the Oral Law on the other (*torah she b'al peh*). Moreover, it is almost always assumed that the earliest Rabbis thought about the provenance of the two *Torahs* in much the same way as the great sages of the Middle Ages—namely, that both a Written Torah and a companion, unwritten Law were given to Moses by God on Mount Sinai. This doctrine has come to be considered almost self-evident in rabbinic religion and is widely thought to be essential to an understanding of the thought of the sages. The classical Rabbis were concerned primarily with the transmission, clarification, and codification of the Oral Law and therefore, it is assumed, derived their authority from the dogma of the revealed Oral Torah, passed through the generations from Sinai. It has been assumed that the classical, rabbinic view of revelation comprehends two revelations in one—*torah she bekhtav* and *torah she b'al*

[*] This is a somewhat revised version of David Weiss Halivni, "The Breaking of the Tablets and the Begetting of the Oral Law, a History of *Torah She be'al Peh*," *Jerusalem Studies in Jewish Thought* 20 (2005): 1–29.

peh—revealed separately, but at one time and in a single encounter, by God to Moses on the mountain.

This study will suggest that the Oral Law in Judaism need not be understood as a separately revealed corpus and that this was not the predominant conception of the Oral Law among the early Rabbis. Rather, the concept of Oral Law and the notion of an Oral Torah were the result of temporal circumstances and fluctuated in prominence throughout time, ebbing and flowing with the vicissitudes of Jewish religious history. Challenged by the early rabbinic predilection for midrash and strengthened by the later mode of Mishnah, the notion of a separate Oral Torah ultimately prevailed because of the diminishment of confidence in the process of exegesis as a means of deriving laws and explanations.

The first portion of this study will set forth the evidence of the traditional sources. We need not revisit at length the conception of revelation preeminent in the Middle Ages since it remains the widely accepted view and the outlook most commonly attributed to the sages. On the other hand, we must consider very carefully what the sages themselves have to say. We will discover that the very concept of a revealed Oral Torah appears hardly at all in the classical rabbinic literature, whereas one would expect the references and allusions to be virtually ubiquitous if this were truly the fundamental doctrine of the Rabbis. We will note that among the very few apparent allusions to revealed Oral Law in the classical sources, most can be interpreted figuratively and nonliterally as statements about the authority of received tradition. What is more, among the allusions that remain—those passages that seem authentically to suggest the revelation of a detailed Oral Law at Sinai—most are attributed to the greatest proponents of the Mishnah, the students of Rabbi Yehudah Hanasi. These statements can be viewed, therefore, as polemics in defense of the self-contained, mishnaic curriculum of Oral Law, at least as much as they are theological comments concerning revelation; and we shall see that such statements were not universally accepted, even as the Rabbi's Mishnah achieved preeminence and canonicity. The idea of a dual Torah—in the sense of two distinct corpora of discrete, explicit, revealed laws—was not a fundamental doctrine of the sages. Rather, the concept developed over time in defense of the curriculum of rabbinic law as it came to be codified and self-contained.

Once we have defended this argument with regard to the classical rabbinic sources, we must suggest a history that will account for the provenance and ascendancy of the idea of *torah she b'al peh*. We will chart a plausible, and indeed probable, history in which interpretation and the transmission of accepted definitions and norms were essential from the outset of the scripturally based tradition. We shall suggest that this Oral Tradition became especially important as the nation, and its Scriptures, were subjected to the tribulations of exile and that the Oral Tradition came to the fore in an essential, guiding, and redeeming role, in the return from Babylonian captivity and the renewed desire for authoritative law. We shall argue that the Oral Tradition in effect took precedence over the scriptural record in the time of return, even as the scriptural Torah was elevated as the visible sign of revelation. The disquieting gap between the Written Torah, as the all-important, visible and scriptural witness to revelation, on the one hand, and the Oral Tradition, as the all-important determinant of actual practice and practical interpretation, on the other hand, was closed by the rabbinic pursuit of midrash. *Halakhah* rooted the Law as it was practiced in the Law as it was written, restoring the sense and the faith that the Law entire had been revealed, practicably, without omission or defect, to Moses at Mount Sinai. However, just as midrash calmed religious unease at the disparity between observed and written Law, midrash itself eventually became a source of pious unease when human virtuosity in exegesis took so prominent a place in the understanding of revelation and its ramifications.

Whatever else may have motivated the genre and the codification of individual statements of law, or *mishnayot* (the unwieldy bulk of exegetically connected rabbinic law and the lack of topical organization in the scripturally bound midrashic curriculum were contributing factors), the rise of the mishnaic mode and of the Mishnah was also a theological and attitudinal phenomenon. Oral Tradition, in and of itself, assumed a new prominence in the Mishnah, and an equally new concept of its provenance began to emerge as well. In opposition to the apparent reliance upon human understanding inherent in midrash, the curriculum of Mishnah suggested that Oral Law could be accepted on its own, with the authority of scriptural revelation.

Concomitantly, certain proponents of Mishnah—most notably the disciples of Rabbi Yehudah Hanasi—began to utter figurative statements about the revelatory authority of Oral Law. Their suggestion eventually gained currency and then prominence. Although it was initially opposed by some of the sages, the concept of the dual and *dually revealed* Torah became the cardinal dogma of rabbinic belief in the Middle Ages and remains current in Judaism today.

The doctrine of dual revelation has become central to rabbinic Judaism. However, we can now appreciate how this doctrine arose in history and trace its rise through the traditional sources, and we can discern a time when it was an embattled and even far-fetched idea. This poses a religious problem to the Jew who wishes to act in accordance with rabbinic Oral Law, to adhere to it as one adheres to God-given Law, and therefore, in effect, to continue to bestow upon it the authority of revelation. If such a Jew is also to read traditional sources with discernment and to appreciate the history of Jewish ideas with intellectual objectivity, then a new theology of the Oral Law is necessary to enable open-minded adherents to cleave to it and trust in it. The final part of this chapter will introduce such a theology, and the result should be of particular interest to modern, observant Jews. We turn first, however, to a careful examination of the sources and history of *torah she b'al peh*, and this study should appeal to all who are interested in the history of Jewish ideas and religion.

PART ONE: THE TRADITIONAL VIEW

To say that the *torah she b'al peh* was revealed by God to Moses, separately from the Written Law but in the same encounter upon Mount Sinai, is to accord to the Oral Law equal authority with the Scriptures as a revelation of God's will. It is to say, as well, that the scriptural Torah, without the *torah she b'al peh*, is incomplete as a record of the revelation to Moses. The fact that we see this conception of revelation commonly held by the rabbinic authorities of the Middle Ages speaks first of all of the reception accorded to the legacy of the classical Rabbis by their medieval heirs. It does not say anything definite about the beliefs of the classical sages themselves, nor does it tell us much about ancient history. Rabbinic thought in its unfolding has been notoriously anachronistic, but to students of religious history it need not seem at all untoward to suggest that the dogmas and doctrines of the Middle Ages should not determine our understanding of the beliefs and ideas of earlier eras.

That the authorities of the Middle Ages contend, in virtual unanimity, that the *torah she b'al peh* was revealed by God to Moses allows us to say something about the status these authorities accorded to their inheritance from the classical Rabbis and about the way in which they championed that inheritance against all who would besmirch it. Through medieval sources we may ascertain the outlook of medieval authorities upon the extrabiblical laws of Judaism. At the same time we should, as a matter of course, be careful to give due consideration to the tendencies, the particular endeavors, and the circumstances of Jewish thought in the Middle Ages before we allow its dogmas to serve as an account of the way in which Torah was experienced and understood by the Rabbis of the classical sources, much less as our history of revelation.

The great commentators of the Middle Ages adopted, developed, and promulgated the concept of an all-inclusive, dual revelation—Written Law and Oral Law, revealed side by side. They conceived of two originally distinct corpora of Torah—laws and their details—revealed distinctly but together and *in toto* to Moses at Mount Sinai. Maimonides, for example, narrates the revelation in his introduction to the Mishnah as follows:

> Know that every commandment that God gave to Moses our Master he gave with its explanation. God would speak the commandment to him, and afterwards speak the explanation, and its deeper meaning, and all that was included by that particular wise verse.

Further on, Maimonides elucidates:

> For example, I may say to you that God dictated to Moses, "In booths shall you dwell seven days," and afterwards gave him to know, may He be exalted, that this matter of booths is incumbent upon males, but not upon females; and that the infirm are not bound by it, nor travelers; and that its roofing must be of material grown from the ground; and not to roof it with wool or silk, and not with useful articles, even such as are made from material grown from the earth, such as mats and clothing; and that one must eat and drink and sleep in it all seven days... And when the Messenger, peace be upon him, came, this commandment and its explanation were given to him—and so too for all the six hundred and thirteen commandments, they and their explanations, the verses written upon scrolls, and the explanation transmitted orally.

In this way, according to Maimonides, every detail necessary to the proper fulfillment of each scriptural command was revealed formally to Moses as part of a second, essential corpus of Law. Of course, Maimonides recognizes a category of rabbinically instituted Law—in the form of decrees and reforms instituted to protect the essential law; and he allows that various ramifications of each commandment that were not received by the people directly from Moses were extrapolated by means of "the thirteen rules that were given to [Moses] on Sinai."

However, with regard to the elementary laws themselves and the explanations needed to follow them, Maimonides recounts,

> When Moses died, peace be upon him, he had already passed to Joshua that which had been given to him of the explanation, and Joshua and the men of his generation contemplated it. And in all that [Joshua] received from [Moses]—he or one of the elders—no argument and no difference of opinion arose in it.

Thus, according to Maimonides, the entire, essential Law, as practiced by the rabbinic Jews of his age, had been given to Moses explicitly, partly in written form and partly in an incorruptible oral tradition. (He in fact enumerates an even forty generations between Moses and R. Ashi, so as to convey the unbrokenness of the chain.) In the context of his time and of his philosophy, one can easily understand Maimonides' desire to assert that the entirety of Jewish law as codified by the classical sages had been revealed directly by God.

In the Kuzari, R. Yehudah Halevi explicitly defends the idea of a dual revelation in contradistinction to the challenge of the Karaites. His ostensibly logical argument for the necessity of revealed Oral Law is suggestive of the mistrust of human interpretation that we shall discuss, in the next part, as a motivating factor in the move from midrash to Mishnah. Relying upon the idea of a God-given Oral Torah, R. Yehudah Halevi deftly turns the Karaite criticism of rabbinic Oral Law, as being human and subjective, back upon the Karaites themselves and argues for the received legacy of the rabbinic sages:

> Al Khazari: All that you say is convincing, because the Scriptures enjoin that there shall be "one Torah and one statute." Should Karaite methods prevail there would be as many different codes as opinions. Not one individual would remain constant to one code. For every day he forms new opinions, increases his knowledge, or meets with someone who refutes him with some argument and converts him to his views. But whenever we find them agreeing, we know that they follow the tradition of one or many of their ancestors. In such a case we should not believe their views and say, "How is it that you agree concerning this regulation, whilst reason allows the word of God to be interpreted in various ways?" If the answer be that this was the opinion of Anan, or Benjamin, or Saul, or others, then they admit the authority of tradition received from people who lived before them, and of the best tradition, viz. that of the sage.

The Karaites, according to R. Yehudah Halevi, "look for a fortress where they can entrench themselves," while the rabbinic Jews, in their reliance on the Oral Law, "lie down on their couches in a place well fortified of old."

R. Moses b. Jacob of Coucy, in the thirteenth century, also affirms the concept of a dual revelation and a revealed Oral Torah in his introduction to the *Sefer Mitzvot Gadol* (*SMaG*). There he writes,

> In truth, God revealed to Moses the explanation of each and every commandment and the measure of each and every matter, and its details, distinctly, and this is the Oral Torah (*torah she b'al peh*), which is the explanation of the Torah and its glory and its splendor. It is for this reason that Moses tarried on the mountain forty days and forty nights and learned [the Torah's] explanations and details. For if Moses had only to give the tablets, he might have done so in an easy hour. God delayed him forty days solely so as to clarify the explanations of the commandments and their details, distinctly.

The author of the *SMaG* derives the necessity of a revealed Oral Law not only from Moses' tarrying on Mount Sinai but also through his appreciation of the fact that the scriptural Torah is insufficient and even self-contradictory as a source of law in the absence of an Oral Torah.

"Had an explanation of the Torah not been given orally," he writes, "the entire Torah would be blindness and sightlessness, for the verses break and contradict one another" and cannot be reconciled without, as he reiterates later on, "the Oral Torah, which is a tradition in the hand of the sages (*ki im mitorah she b'al peh shehi masoret beyad chakhamim*)."

The Torah, according to the *SMaG*, "is great and mighty in the extreme, so that the Scriptures [alone] cannot contain it (*asher haketav lo yachilenah*)." This assertion on the part of the *SMaG* is crucial to our understanding of the characteristically post-Talmudic and medieval view of the Oral Torah, as distinct from the predominating view among the early sages. According to R. Moses b. Jacob of Coucy—as he seeks to demonstrate at length, through many examples in the introduction to the *SmaG*—the letters, words, and verses of the *torah she bekhtav* are inherently insufficient, and even problematic, without a separate, God-given *torah she b'al peh*. By contrast, as we shall see in the next part, the early Rabbis who were proponents of midrash worked to demonstrate that the whole of the Law was comprised in the Scriptures, if only one knew how to look into their depths.

Before proceeding to the next part, it should be noted that the authorities of the Middle Ages were not oblivious to this function of midrash: that the classic rabbinic sources deduced many laws, including essential ones, by means of scriptural exegesis. The medieval authorities did not obscure, nor did they seek to deny, ingenious rabbinic *midrashim*. They did not conceive of these *midrashim* as sources of the Law, however, but only as efforts to discover hints and allusions to a separate Oral Torah within the text of the *torah she bekhtav*. Their conception was similar to the classical rabbinic notion of *asmakhta, or "support"*: that a scriptural verse may be cited merely in support of a rabbinic law, rather than as its revealed source. It must be noted, at the same time, that Maimonides reserves the term *asmakhta* for what he considers a more inferior kind of linkage to the Scriptures: one in which the scriptural passage in question does not truly allude to the Oral Law but is merely designated by human minds as a kind of mnemonic. In any event, it is clear that by the Middle Ages, Jewish legal and intellectual leaders had distanced the observed Law as far as possible from human agency. The concept of the dual revelation and the revealed Oral Torah left no room for human involvement in the deduction or explanation of any truly essential point of the Law. The *torah she b'al peh* was regarded as a corpus unto itself, originally revealed to Moses on Mount Sinai and embedded piecemeal in the textual legacy of the classical Rabbis. By arguing for the revelatory status of a distinct, Oral Law, the medieval religious leaders spoke to the religious sensibilities of their times, presenting a picture of a complete and comprehensive revelation, flowing from a source essentially separate and distant from human reasoning and insight. For the earliest Rabbis, the religious problem to be solved was exactly the opposite. For them, an oral tradition that dictated authoritative practice needed grounding in the scriptural Torah. The urgency of that need—which was the impelling force behind rabbinic midrash—can be understood only when we realize that among those early Rabbis, for the most part, the *torah she bekhtav* alone was regarded as the revealed Torah of Mount Sinai. We turn, next, to examine the textual evidence for this early rabbinic belief.

PART TWO: THE ORAL TORAH
IN THE THOUGHT OF THE SAGES

For the most part, the founding sages of the rabbinic movement did not conceive of *torah she b'al peh* as an independently revealed corpus, as was assumed in the Middle Ages. Such a notion of Oral Torah does not find convincing support in the *oeuvre* of the earliest Rabbis. The notion of revealed Oral Law appears only extremely infrequently in classical rabbinic literature—certainly not as often as one would expect if it were really a central doctrine of the sages—and most of the apparent allusions can be explained as figurative turns of speech rather than dogmas. Even the suggestion of a dual Torah is only very rarely to be found in classical rabbinic literature.

A very few *tannaitic* passages allude to the concept, and the term *torah she b'al peh*, as such, occurs only once in a statement attributed to an Amora, and that one reference, in *Yoma* 28b, is not found in the manuscripts, nor in the commentary of Rabbenu Chananel. Our printed editions of *Yoma* 28b read,

> Rava, and some say R. Ashi said: Abraham our Father fulfilled even the commandment of *eruv tavshilin* ["mixed (cooked) dishes" prepared prior to Jewish holiday that precedes Shabbat], as it is written [since he has hearkened to] my Torahs (*torotai*)—both the Written Torah and the Oral Torah (*torah she b'al peh*).

However, manuscripts of *Yoma* read *divrei soferim* ["dictates of the sages," or rabbinic law that is derived from the Written Torah but not explicit in it] instead of *torah she b'al peh*, and so too does the parallel comment of Rabbenu Chananel. This evidence suggests that our text was modified, either intentionally or inadvertently, at a time when *torah she b'al peh* had become a common concept and the natural partner and rejoinder to *torah she bekhtav*. It seems not to have been so in the time when the amoraic statement of *Yoma* 28b was composed.

Three *tannaitic* accounts seemingly refer to a dual Torah—Written and Oral. The first, in *Shabbat* 31a, is the story of the prospective convert who asks of Shammai, "How many *torot* do you [Israel] possess (*kamah torot yesh lakhem*)?" The reply, "Two: one in writing and one oral," seems a clear indication that a concept of *torah she b'al peh* was current among the early Rabbis. On closer inspection, however, this source cannot be taken as evidence for a belief in revealed Oral Law. The prospective convert is skeptical and desires only to learn the Written Law, whereupon Hillel teaches him the beginning of the Hebrew Alphabet—forward on the first day but in reverse on the following day. When the prospective convert expresses astonishment at the reversal, Hillel, in quiet triumph, responds, "Did you not rely upon me [with regard to the order]? Then rely upon me with regard to the oral [Torah] also!" This story is manifestly about the need for a chain of teachers to transmit a tradition of *reading* the Scriptures—that is to say, a tradition of *interpretation*. Were it not for the prominence of the idea in the literature of the Middle Ages, we might never read this story as alluding to a formal Oral Law revealed to Moses at Sinai. Hillel asks that the prospective convert rely upon him as a purveyor of tradition and explanation, but that is surely not to say that he shares Maimonides' concept of the dual revelation at Sinai. What the prospective convert found objectionable was not oral revelation but rabbinic exegesis.

In fact, it is fascinating to note that a much later redaction of this same story, in *Avot Derabbi Natan* (*nuscha bet*), puts the question of the prospective convert rather differently. There, he is said to have asked, "How many *torot* were given to you from heaven? (*kamah torot nitnu lakhem min hashamayim?*)?" *Nuscha bet* of *Avot Derabbi Natan* has been dated to the ninth century.[1] So this very poignant (even polemical) variation from the early to the later version of the question may serve to define a chronological divide between a time when revealed Oral Law was not a common concept and the question was only how many Torahs (*torot*) Israel had, and a time when the idea was read into earlier sources wherever possible.

The second *tannaitic* allusion to a dual Torah is a stronger indication that a concept of revealed Oral Law may have had some currency among the Tannaim, but again the conclusion is not necessary. This source, in the *Sifra* on *Bechukotai*, comments upon the passage, "these are the rules (*chukim*) and the judgements (*mishpatim*) and the laws (*torot*) which God gave on Mount Sinai by the hand of Moses" and reads as follows:

> "The *chukim*"—these are the *midrashot*; "and the *mishpatim*"—these are the rulings (*dinim*); "and the *torot*"—this teaches that two *Torot* were given to Israel, one in writing and one orally.
>
> Said R. Akiba: And were [only] two *torot* given to Israel? Many *torot* were given to them, as it is written, "This is the *torah* of the whole offering," "This is the *torah* of the meal offering," "This is the *torah* of the guilt offering," . . .
>
> "Which God gave"—between Himself and Israel—Moses merited to be made an emissary between Israel and their Father in Heaven.
>
> "On Mount Sinai, by the hand of Moses"—this teaches that the Torah was given with its rules and details and explanations (*halakhot, perushehem vedikdukehem*) through Moses from Mount Sinai.

Here again, we may interpret the "two *torot*" as the Written Torah and the Torah of *interpretation*. *Perushim* ("explanations") and *dikdukim* ("exacting details") certainly connoted human exegetical and judicial activity to tannaitic authors. Thus, the statement "Two *torot* were given to Israel, one in writing and one orally" may indicate that an Oral Torah was, and is, given to Israel by means of exegesis and interpretation—which would be in keeping with the spirit of the *tannaitic* times, as we shall see. In the same vein we may also explain the last portion of this passage—"that the Torah was given with its rules and details and explanations through Moses from Mount Sinai." A similar statement is found in the *Sifra* at the beginning of *Behar* (quoted by both Rashi and Rambam): "All of the commandments were stated with their general principles, details, and specifics (*kelalehen, peratehen, vedikdukehen*) from Sinai."

However, the *Sifra* in *Bechukotai* does not say that the details and explanations of the Torah were given *to* Moses on Mount Sinai but rather that they were given *through* Moses from Sinai. It may be that Moses, in this *halakhic* reading, is cast as the rabbinic sage par excellence, able to perceive and to teach the deeper nuances of the Torah and thereby to serve as an intermediary between Israel and God. That implicit assertion may account for the otherwise rather simple observation that Moses achieved the status of "emissary between Israel and their Father in Heaven." This entire *halakhic* passage might actually define what it meant to be such an emissary in the view of the early sages: namely, to be able to perceive and deliver to the people the *halakhot, dikdukim,* and *perushim*—the interpretations and the rulings—emanating from the revealed, scriptural Torah.

In present-day rabbinic parlance, it is not astonishing to hear *perushim* and *dikdukim* spoken of as categories of revealed Law from Sinai, but that parlance is heavily influenced by the concepts of the Middle Ages. In the time of the early sages, by contrast, the terms *perushim* and *dikdukim* indicated the essential activities of the Rabbis—interpretation and practical judgment. If the Tannaim conceived of a second, unwritten Torah, it was most likely a Torah arising, or at least deriving its authority, from their own activity—as the story of the prospective convert, considered above, indicates. That may well be the message of the *Sifra* as well.

It is well worth noting that the allusion to two *torot* arouses astonishment, perhaps even confusion (or feigned confusion?), on the part of R. Akiba. R. Akiba's almost facile scriptural observation—with its seemingly stubborn refusal to comprehend or admit what is meant by "two *torot*" in the foregoing interpretation—may actually be shrewdly calculated as an objection to the interpretation that suggests a dual revelation. Though we cannot say so with certainty, R. Akiba, as a great proponent of midrashic interpretation, may even be reacting here against what he perceived to be the birth of a stifling and disempowering concept of duality in revelation.

We should also note, in connection with R. Akiba's interjection in the *Sifra* of *Bechukotai*, that we find R. Akiba elsewhere on the side of exegetical derivation, while his interlocutors argue for the supremacy of received tradition. In *Niddah* 72b, for example, the following response follows R. Akiba's exegetical proof for the correct measure of oil to be brought by the nazirite (based upon the reduplication of the word *beshemen*):

> Said R. Elazar b. Azariah to R. Akiba: Even if you argue from the reduplication of *beshemen* all day long (*afilu atah marbeh beshemen kol hayom kulo*) I shall not listen to you; but the half *log* of oil for a thanksgiving offering and a quarter log of wine for the nazirite and the eleven days between menstrual periods are *halakhah lemoshe misinai* ["Oral Law given to Moses on Sinai]!

First of all, we should note that R. Elazar b. Azariah's inclusion of "a quarter log of wine" and "the eleven days between menstrual periods" in this discussion suggests that there are only a very few, particular laws that he would identify as "the Oral Law passed down from Sinai," *halakhah lemoshe misinai*—perhaps only the three he mentions here. That is, even if we take the expression literally, R. Elazar b. Azariah is certainly not arguing for a comprehensive, revealed Oral Law as imagined in the Middle Ages. He seems to be saying that certain laws are known to be hard and fast as matters of tradition, while other laws are susceptible to the give-and-take of rabbinic exegesis and disputation. Further, it is not certain that R. Elazar b. Azariah means for his words to be taken literally at all. Rather, it seems probable that *halakhah lemoshe misinai* was used by the sages as a polemical hyperbole, asserting long-standing and undisputed tradition over and against rabbinic deduction. Used rhetorically, the term probably does not indicate a theological dogma, and it certainly should not be assumed to represent the dogma of the comprehensive, revealed Oral Law that we find in later thought.

A polemical and hyperbolic, rather than literal, usage of *halakhah lemoshe misinai* seems to be in evidence in the following exchange from the Mishnah of *Yadaim* 4:3:

[The sages] voted and taught: [residents of] Amon and Moav must tithe the tithe of the poor in the seventh year. Then, when R. Yosi b. Dormaskit came to R. Eliezer in Lod, the latter asked him, "What new rulings had you in the *beit halakhah* today?" He replied, "They voted and taught: [residents of] Amon and Moav must tithe the tithe of the poor in the seventh year." [Thereupon] R. Eliezer cried and said, "'The counsel of the Lord is with them that fear Him, and to them He will reveal His covenant!' (Psalms 25:14) Go and tell them, 'Think nothing of your voting! I learned from R. Yochanan b. Zakkai who heard from his teacher, and his teacher from his teacher, even unto *halakhah lemoshe misinai* that [residents] of Amon and Moav must tithe the tithe of the poor in the seventh year!'"

It is clear that R. Eliezer's admonition "Think nothing of your voting" is delivered with regard to the particular *halakhah* in question. It is not intended as a general, theological statement about revelation but rather polemically emphasizes that this specific ruling is far from an innovation in R. Eliezer's generation. Elsewhere, R. Eliezer is not opposed to rabbinic reasoning and deliberation. As is already noted by medieval and modern commentators, the fact that the lands of Amon and Moab were conquered only after Moses' death strengthens the argument that R. Eliezer is not implying an historical, Mosaic revelation.

Resuming our search for allusions in *tannaitic* sources to a doctrine of two Torahs (*torot*), we come, finally, to the *Sifre Deuteronomy Piska* 351, which is parallel to, and apparently carried over from, the source just considered in the *Sifra*. The *Sifre* comments upon the scriptural blessing to the tribe of Levi, "They shall teach Your statutes to Jacob and Your laws to Israel," saying, "This teaches that two *torot* were given to Israel, one in writing, the other orally." We should note that the *Sifre* reads "*torotekha*" (plural), whereas our Masoretic reading is "*toratekha*" (singular). Again, as in the *Sifra* on *Bechukotai* and the story in *Shabbat* 31a, this *tannaitic* passage probably speaks of an Oral Torah arising from and composed of *interpretations*. Indeed that is the traditional role of the Tribe of Levi in the Scriptures and in the historical conception of the Rabbis—providing interpretations of the Law to Israel.

PART THREE: THE MISHNAH

The emergence of Rabbi Yehudah Hanasi's Mishnah and of the genre of Mishnah on the rabbinic landscape reflects a tendency toward Oral

Law presented without accompanying exegesis. For whatever practical, historical, and religious reasons (and we shall consider the religious reasons in the next part), there was a call, toward the close of the second century C.E., for a concise Mishnah of *halakhot*, mostly without motive clauses and *midrashim*. The Mishnah's seemingly freestanding, independent Oral Law, divorced for the most part from midrash, strengthened (and perhaps relied upon) a gradually emerging notion of an originally separate and revealed Oral Torah, given to Moses alongside the Scriptures.

Although, as we have noted, the term *torah she b'al peh* is not used by the Amoraim, the idea of a revealed Oral Torah is promulgated in three Amoraic sources. Remarkably, all three sources can be linked to sages who were the disciples of Rabbi Yehudah Hanasi. This is unlikely to be a coincidence and very probably bespeaks a theological and narrative defense of the emergent, canonical Mishnah on the part of its greatest adulators.

The first of these sources, in *Berakhot* 5a, reads as follows:

> Said R. Shimon b. Lakish: What is the meaning of the verse, "And I gave to you the tablets of stone, and the law, and the commandment, which I had written, to teach them?" "The tablets"—those are the ten commandments; "law" (*torah*)—that is Scripture; "and the commandment"—that is Mishnah; "which I had written"—that refers to the prophets; "to teach them"—that is *Gemara*; thus [this verse] teaches that all of them were given to Moses from Sinai.

We should note that the plain sense of the verse, which speaks of the various laws that God had written, is undermined by Resh Lakish's interpretation in favor of a conception of revelation that has Mishnah and even *Gemara* given to Moses at Sinai. Elsewhere I have argued at length that the Rabbis referred to *Gemara*—or Talmud, as we read in uncensored editions—as their characteristic mode of disputation and elucidation, the practice through which final opinions and decisions were reached.[2] This being so, we can appreciate that Resh Lakish's statement is a radically maximalistic conception of revelation extended to include *Gemara*. The statement was probably offered polemically, perhaps even aiming, through overstatement, to secure a place for Mishnah in the canon of revelation—R. Yehudah Hanasi's Mishnah in particular.

The second Amoraic allusion to revealed Oral Law, also attributable to a disciple of R. Yehudah Hanasi, is the famous passage in *Talmud*

Yerushalmi Peah 2:4 in which R. Joshua b. Levi asserts that even that which a diligent student will one day speak before his teacher was already revealed to Moses on Mount Sinai. We should note, again, that this is an extreme statement, even out of keeping with the concept of revealed Oral Law current in the Middle Ages. The passage in the *Yerushalmi* suggests that Moses was accorded a glimpse of the entire future course of rabbinic learning—an idea with some currency in rabbinic lore. This conception is distinct from the formal corpus of revealed and transmitted Oral Law imagined by the authorities of the Middle Ages.

The third Amoraic allusion comes in *Megillah* 19b through R. Yochanan's interpretation of the Deuteronomic passage concerning the tablets of stone—"and on them was written all the words that the Lord spoke to you at the Mountain." R. Yochanan says this teaches that God revealed to Moses details of the Law (*dikduke torah* and *dikduke soferim*) as well as "that which the *soferim* [scribes] were one day to innovate," for example, the reading of the scroll of Esther. This is another extreme statement, once again out of keeping with the expansive yet definite and formal conception of the revealed Oral Law current in the Middle Ages. Maimonides, for example, acknowledged that certain later points of the law, certain innovations, and measures enacted to protect the law were added by subsequent, wise interpreters of the legacy of revelation. Moreover, while later rabbinic literature lent the holidays of Purim and Chanukah some revealed status, responsibility for both the holidays and their observances was more commonly assigned to the leaders of each generation, in accordance with Scripture's admonition that Israel follow its leaders' words. R. Yochanan's portrayal of the revelation to Moses is thus broader and more general than the dogma of revealed Oral Torah that we find in the Middle Ages.

These three *midrashic* accounts of revelation may have been offered to defend the Mishnah itself, as a curriculum of independent oral law presented, for the most part, without exegetical justification. The accounts assure students that the Oral teachings to which they devote so many hours of study and effort are as much a part of the legacy of Sinai as the Scriptures. These accounts may therefore be read as apologies for an independent, oral tradition rather than as literal narratives of what was revealed at Sinai. As R. Abraham, the son of Maimonides, suggests, they may have been offered to encourage and inspire students of rabbinic tradition, to give them a sense of the value

of their curriculum and a sense of their own importance in the fulfillment of revelation.[3] We should not, therefore, read these passages
as evidence that the classic sages already maintained the medieval
dogma of the revealed Oral Law. If, after all, the absolute entirety of
the Law, to which the passage in *Y. Peah* 2:4 clearly alludes, was not
only revealed to Moses but also transmitted verbatim from him
through the generations, what need would there ever have been for
the *talmid vatic* ("advanced student") portrayed in this passage? The
Yerushalmi clearly speaks here of a proleptic glimpse, not a transmitted legacy. The medieval conception of *halakhah lemoshe misinai* is at
once more limited and more soberly intended than the Amoraic
speculations on revelation.

One may object that, in *Y. Peah* 2:4, R. Yehoshua b. Levi includes *aggadot* among the aspects of Torah revealed to Moses at Sinai. But his
claim cannot be meant as a dogma, for elsewhere R. Yehoshua b. Levi
seems opposed to aggadah, or at least to raising aggadah to the level
of Scripture and other tradition.[4] In sum, *Peah* 2:4 seems to imply that
the scriptural Torah was revealed to Moses along with a glimpse or assurance of the faithful exegesis that would ensue. R. Abraham ben
Rambam's supposition that this passage does not refer to transmitted
Oral Law is echoed in the introduction to the Mishnah of the Tosafot
Yom Tov, who suggests that Moses was given this insight as a vision of
the future but not as a legacy to transmit formally to that future (*"bederekh reyah velo bederekh masora"*).

In sum, statements by these three disciples of Rabbi Yehudah
Hanasi do not constitute a formal dogma of "the Oral Law passed
down from Sinai," as it was later conceived by medieval authorities. At
the same time, these statements are indications of a tendency that
emerged in the Amoraic period and increased through the medieval
and modern periods: as confidence in the human activity of exegesis
waned, even in the time of the sages, scholars began gradually to conceive of an originally separate, revealed Oral Law and of an oral tradition that might be accepted on its own authority.

PART FOUR: THE HISTORY OF ORAL LAW

The sages say, "If the tablets had not been broken, Torah would not
have been forgotten in Israel" (*Eruvin* 54a). By the same token, we
might say, "If the tablets had not been broken, the Oral Torah would

not exist." The storied neglect and disregard that led to Moses' breaking of the tablets and the similar neglect that, in the tradition's terms, resulted in exile and captivity made it necessary for Israel to live with a fractured and reconstituted Torah, assembled from the shards of the tablets, so to speak, fraught with ambiguity and uncertainty and even lacunae and in need of augmentation and human repair. Either the Oral Law is, as Maimonides suggests, the result of a perfect and perfectly preserved revelation, or, as this essay will suggest, the Oral Law is largely the result of an historical need for explication and interpretation of the Scriptures associated with revelation.

To keep our footing in the rabbinic tradition, we may begin a history of the Oral Law by noting certain suggestions, within the tradition itself, that the Scriptures revealed at Sinai were more complete than those which survive in our hands. First of all, we must acknowledge the possibility of a more extensive written tradition and the possibility that certain elements of the Oral Law aim to compensate for a disappearance of material from the Scriptures over time. R. Saadya Gaon suggests (in *Ginzei Kedem II*) that certain areas of the Law were originally more complete and more explicit in the Torah given by Moses to the people. He comments,

> In the Torah of Moses we find many matters written at length as, for example, the building of the tabernacle, the pericope of priestly assignments, the census of Israel, and the dedication of the altar, and—to differentiate—the laws concerning discharges are written in extreme brevity, and the laws of calendrical intercalation are all bound up in the single word *"aviv"* ["Spring"] alone, which would be extremely astonishing were we not to posit that *these laws too were once written in clear detail, but are no longer with us in writing and are, instead, transmitted orally.*

R. Saadya Gaon probably bases his words on the following comment found in *Midrash Shir Hashirim Rabbah* 5:12:[5]

> Just as in the sea, between each and every great wave there are small ripples, so too between each and every utterance [were] details and signs (*otot*) of Torah written.

Such suggestions, within the rabbinic tradition itself, remind and encourage us to consider the gaps and the inconsistencies that may have arisen in the Scriptures over time. One role of Oral Law, and one motivating goal of Oral Law, was surely to address such gaps and inconsistencies. We can imagine that oral traditions—more or less formal recollections—may have survived among some pious few even as the masses neglected the Scriptures and allowed the Written Torah to become maculate.

Principally, we may conceive of two kinds of scriptural material that may have gone missing from the scriptural record while remaining alive in the memory and the life of the people. The first may be termed *interpretation* and *definition*, that is, additional explication and detail— more refined calendrical information, finer particulars of practices such as divorce and Shabbat, and such crucial qualifications as *pikuach nefesh*, or times when the religious law can be abrogated to "save human life." When, for example, the *Sifra* in *Bechukotai* says that *midrashot* were revealed to Moses at Sinai, it most likely means that these kinds of additional explication and detail were initially part of the Scriptures themselves. We may imagine that a second kind of missing material concerned broad accounts of major institutions— such as *nisuch hamayim* (the libation of water on the holiday of Sukkot) and the *aravah* rite (striking the "willow branch" on Hoshanah Rabbah). In any event we must admit and wonder—as do the sages—that many essential and prominent elements of ancient law and practice are not included in the Written Torah. Some of these may once have been written.

Even without the deterioration of the Scriptures, there must have been an immediate need for explanation as soon as the Written Torah was accepted. It had to be taught, for example, that "You shall surely release it with him" (*azov ta'azov imo*, Exodus 23:5) pertains only when the owner helps along and that "If brethren dwell together" (*ki yeshvu achim yachdav*, Deuteronomy 25:5) applies only when all the brothers were alive and together—not to mention that the details of Sabbath and Festival observance had to be authoritatively standardized and promulgated. Whatever oral traditions may have accompanied the Written Law in the wilderness and in the First Temple period, the need for explanation and guidance was especially acute in the time of Ezra, the time of return from Babylonian captivity, which may be seen as the point at which Israel as a whole accepted the Torah.

We may imagine that a relatively small remnant of faithful adherents to the Torah—prophets, priests and scribes, and their closest followers—provided definitions and explications to the newly desirous nation in the time of its return from Babylonian captivity. We may also imagine that these leaders relied upon unwritten tradition—in effect, Oral Law—as they purveyed such necessary information. We have no assurance that such Oral Law was preserved perfectly throughout the ages of idolatry and exile as a faithful reflection of the earliest adherence to the Torah, but it was preserved well enough—and, in any case, presented authoritatively enough—to serve as a guide, and even sometimes a corrective, in implementing the Scriptures anew.

Some of these unwritten traditions may have been unwritten from the very beginning. We certainly need not imagine, as did the medieval thinkers, that this unwritten Law was revealed at Sinai as a complete, detailed corpus for oral transmission. On the one hand, certain terms and institutions may have been well understood by the ancient Israelites without a need for more detailed scriptural information, thus instantly becoming part of an adjunct, oral, or even physical and material tradition. On the other hand, from the beginning, there was a provision for judges and priests to interpret and apply the Law to various circumstances as they arose. In these ways an Oral Torah—in the sense of a living tradition of interpretation and application—must have grown up around the Scriptures from the very outset.

One might argue that, before Josiah's reign (639–608 B.C.E.) when, according to the biblical narrative, the Torah was forgotten (II Kings 22–23; II Chronicles 34), the people relied primarily on oral traditions—that is, to whatever extent they maintained nonidolatrous practices. If so, however, these oral traditions could not have been the comprehensive Oral Law that the medieval writers imagined to have been revealed directly to Moses at Sinai. As depicted in the biblical narratives, the people could hardly have neglected the principal tenets and practices mandated at Sinai if, at the same time, they also preserved detailed guidelines for their implementation. In his Introduction to the *Mishneh Torah*, Maimonides counts forty uninterrupted generations of transmission, teacher to student, from Moses to R. Ashi, entirely ignoring the biblical account of the Torah's being forgotten. If there were such an Oral Law, even a single generation of forgetting and broken transmission would have led to its demise. If a detailed, revealed Oral Law of particulars, such as Maimonides imagines, had been forgotten along with the neglected Scriptures, it could never have been reproduced once the Scriptures were rediscovered; it would have been lost forever. It is no wonder that the biblical account of the Torah's being forgotten is hardly mentioned at all in medieval commentary and that one commentator who does mention the story, R. Nissim Gaon, inveighs against a literal interpretation.[6] However, if we understand Oral Law as a developing legacy of explanation, dependent on the Scriptures, then we can say that once the Written Torah was rediscovered and recognized, Oral Law would have reemerged alongside it.

The religious leaders of the Return from Exile provided the best possible scriptural Torah for Israel to receive in the wake of its exilic catastrophe. They also provided the information and guidance that was necessary to understand and to live according to those Scriptures—or, more precisely, according to the divine covenant for which those Scriptures stood as a written testament and record. However, from the very time of canonization, it must have been apparent to the faithful that there was disparity between the Torah as it was to be lived according to the authority of tradition and the Scriptures as they stood recovered from the flames of destruction and desolation.

We may then speculate that the religious sensibilities of the faithful were set on edge by this disparity between practice and Scripture, that is, between the fullness and detail of the Oral Law and the paucity and ambiguity of the Written. This discomfort gave rise to an effort to prove that the details of the Law as it was lived were not only rooted in the scriptural Law but also actually *present* in the Scriptures, in detail, if only the Scriptures were read correctly. This effort gave rise to an unprecedented, inventive reading of the Written Torah through which subtle indications and coded references to laws not explicit in the Scriptures were discovered. Early traces of such an effort may be discerned in the Hebrew Bible itself, and these, we may infer, engendered what eventually become rabbinic *midrash halakhah* ("legal interpretation"). By the same token, both scriptural and unwritten law were continuously brought to bear upon new circumstances and situations, generating still more extrascriptural law that called for grounding in the Written Torah. Verses were linked by means of *halakhah* to the Law as it moved in the life of the people and in the minds and memories of the religious leaders, giving the impression, and the assurance, that the details of the covenantal way of life emanated directly from the scriptural text of the covenant itself. In this way, differences of opinion were resolved with regard to the fine points of observance, and discrepancies among various factions or schools of practice were resolved, or at least debated, through readings of the Written Torah and efforts to discern its subtle signs and allusions. There was, as we have said, a biblical precedent for this endeavor; in II Chronicles 35:13, for example, we see an effort to resolve contradictory Scriptures through innovative reading. Then, however, the extent and sophistication of this creative approach to the Scriptures grew exponentially. Skilled practitioners of this newly refined art mined the Written Torah for more and more subtle evidences of long-standing customs and teachings, developing quasi-scientific principles of exegesis and applying them with great inventiveness and audacity.

In this way, *midrashim* in support of one or another practice became associated with the name of this or that Rabbi, although for the most part the practices predated these sages by many years. From the early stages of rabbinic exegesis, even as attributed *midrashim* proliferated and became the predominant form of codified extrascriptural law, an idea remained, embedded in the spiritual fabric and history of Judaism, that authoritative, received tradition must rule over scriptural searching and exegetical prowess and even determine its conclusions. Accordingly, while *halakhah* flourished and multiplied in the early rabbinic generations, there remained a cardinal belief, at least among some,[7] that a practice or an answer received through an ancient and venerable channel of transmission was more important—quite probably more authentic—than a decision or solution achieved through exegetical innovation: "If this is a *halakhah* we will accept it, but if it is an exegetical inference there may be a rebuttal" (*im halakhah nekabel veim ledin yesh teshuvah*).[8] Competing *midrashim*, supporting rival practices or rulings, could and indeed had to be weighed one against the other when no one definitive answer from tradition was known or when the issue was a novel one, not directly addressed in the religious legacy of the Torah's application. However, many leading sages of this golden age of rabbinic exegesis—traditionalists—clung to the principle that the legacy of inherited praxis and teaching, even where not linked to impressive *midrashim*, should take precedence over fresh exegetical derivations, however compelling in their artistry and insight. Even so, the earliest rabbinic generations were definitively the epoch of *halakhah*, and *midrash halakhah* became the chief manner and vehicle through which detailed religious law was arranged and transmitted in the generations preceding the composition and compilation of the mishnayot.

We can discern the spirit of *halakhah* and precedent for this rabbinic activity in the period immediately before the rise of the Rabbis. For example, as Lawrence Schiffman has noted, the legal materials of the Dead Sea sect are, to a large extent, grounded in and justified through a process of scriptural exegesis. Schiffman writes,

The sect divided the law into two categories—the *nigleh* "revealed," and the *nistar*, "hidden." The revealed laws were known to all Israel, for they were manifest in Scripture, but the hidden laws were known only to the sect and were revealed solely through sectarian exegesis.[9]

We can detect a similar attitude toward rabbinic Oral Law—termed the *mysterion* of Israel[10]—in the thought of the early sages. Beyond examining how the various genres of legal writing found at Qumran are founded upon exegesis, Schiffman draws our attention, in particular, to the following passage as an illustration of how law is justified through scriptural interpretation. Drawn from the *Rule of the Community*, thought to be a central document of the sect, the passage discusses the commitment of a new member to the sect:

> And he shall establish by a covenant upon himself to separate from all men of iniquity who walk in the path of evil. For they have not been reckoned in His covenant, for they did not search and did not study His laws, to know the secrets (*nistarot*) in which they erred, incurring guilt, and the revealed (*niglot*) they did (violate) defiantly.[11]

Within the rabbinic movement, a similar attitude prevailed regarding adherence to the Oral Law. Those who denied the authority of the Oral Tradition denied not only the Law as received through the generations but also—after the rise of rabbinic midrash—the Law as discerned through correct and specialized reading of the Scriptures.

The surge of midrash initiated by the early rabbinic sages became so strong in the ensuing generations that the impulse to find scriptural indications of accepted Law and interpretation even displaced certain tannaitic assumptions about scriptural diction and its implications. The Mishnah of *Baba Kama* 5:7, for example, reads,

> [Not only] the ox, [but] likewise all beasts, are included in the biblical injunctions concerning falling into a pit, and keeping away from Mount Sinai, and double repayment, and returning lost property, and likewise are all animals and fowl [included]. If so, why are only "ox" and "donkey" written [in these cases]? The Scripture spoke of the case commonly encountered [implying the rest].

We might call this a moderate *midrashic* reading of Scripture, built on the assumption that "Scripture spoke of the common case," which means that holy writ, like human speech, sometimes makes reference to particular examples in speaking of general principles. This stands in sharp contrast to parallel texts in the *Tosefta, midrash halakhah*, and *Gemara*. In the *Tosefta* and midrash *halakhah*, R. Akiba and R. Yishmael go to great lengths to demonstrate, by means of minute exegeses, how other animals are included in these scriptural injunctions. The *Gemara* that is attached to this Mishnah in *Baba Kama* 54b goes even further to subvert the Mishnah's self-sufficient claim, resorting again and again to scriptural hints to prove that other animals are included in each of the injunctions mentioned. In sum, while the Mishnah appears to obviate the need for further exegetical justification of the accepted interpretations, the impulse toward *halakhic* justification generates a very different sense, that each particular detail of the Law as practiced was incomplete or insufficient without its own particular linkage to the Scriptures. That sense accounts in large part for the explosion of *halakhah* that is evident in the classical rabbinic sources.

In all probability, two factors led to the eventual decline of *halakhah* and the move toward Mishnah with its terse formulation of the law, mostly devoid of Scripture and motive clause. From a practical point of view, there must have been a call for a topically organized, manageable, and definitive curriculum of religious law to pass authoritatively from generation to generation. The complete and elaborate range of *midrash halakhah* must have been too vast, unwieldy, and unstructured with regard to topic to have continued to serve as an effective program of learning or as a resource and guide for the application of the law. However, just as important, there seems also to have been a loss of confidence in the art of exegesis.

Paradoxically, considering its initial motivations, *halakhah* itself may have led to a sense of uncertainty or indeterminacy. To be sure, *halakhah* grounded familiar religious practice in the Scriptures, but as an art of interpretation *halakhah* also raised the unsettling possibility that alternative legal conclusions and interpretations might be equally tenable. Just as the laconic, vague, and sometimes contradictory Scriptures had once troubled religious sensibilities because of their difference and occasional divergence from observed law, now the vast *oeuvre* of attributed *halakhah*, which linked common, covenantal practices and regulations with the names and interpretations of living and recently living human beings, disquieted the pious mind no less.

Emerging in the place of *halakhah*, as a curriculum and eventually as a predominating mode of framing and understanding the Oral Law, was a genre composed of serial *halakhot*—attributed to named Rabbis, it is true, but (for the most part) attached to their names because they conveyed these teachings and not because they derived them through exegesis. Even though these Rabbis had very often produced such derivations and even though their scriptural interpretations do appear, albeit infrequently, within the genre of Mishnah, their exegetical endeavors were predominantly omitted in the formulation of *mishnayot*. Oral Law was severed once more from the scriptural Torah. In the genre of Mishnah—as distinct from the source material from which its rulings were culled—received tradition made a bid for renewed supremacy over inventive reading. As a result, the very art of scriptural exegesis waned—at least in the realm of jurisprudence—as rulings, divorced from their erstwhile proofs, were presented anew as received traditions. The mode and genre of Mishnah—with its repetition of extrascriptural *halakhah*, almost entirely on its own, without recourse to exegesis—must have helped to restore the sense that divine law, rather than human endeavor, was at the center of tradition.

The Mishnah's separation of Oral Law from Scripture must have been accompanied by a shift in the theology of revelation. As we have suggested earlier, the theological and doctrinal consequences of the transition to Mishnah found expression in such statements as those of the three disciples of R. Yehudah Hanasi (the mishnaic compiler par excellence). Those statements suggest that a revelation resembling, if not identical to *mishnah*—or, rather, to the Mishnah—was granted along with the Scriptures to Moses at Sinai. In this sense, Mishnah and the theology of Mishnah functioned as a theological corrective to the hazards of human *halakhah*. Where *halakhah* had calmed religious unease by assuring the pious that the Law entire sprung from the scriptural Torah, Mishnah and its dogmatic defense did the same by insisting that all Law—written and oral—originated in revelation.

That dogma is the theological and doctrinal foundation of the medieval discussions of revelation and rabbinic law that we discussed earlier—those of the Rambam, the introduction to the *SMaG*, and the Kuzari. For those commentators, rabbinic law is authoritative because it is the content of Sinaitic revelation. To be sure, this claim required elaborate and even tortuous defense in the face of a legacy of rabbinic texts featuring disagreement and argumentation. The medieval sources offer such defenses, arriving by various pathways to the shared conclusion that the essential, authoritative rulings of the Rabbis were revealed at Sinai. While the challenge of such opponents as the Karaites goaded the early medieval thinkers to defend the Oral Law and its divine origin all the more vehemently, we have seen that forces and tendencies within Judaism itself were quite sufficient to precipitate this theological movement.

Remarkably, the tendency toward the preternaturalization and elevation of rabbinic law to the status of divine revelation did not end with the Middle Ages or even, for the most part, with the rise of the Age of Reason in the world surrounding Judaism. To the contrary, that tendency charged onward in Jewish orthodoxy and continues to do so even today. The tendency has led to such extreme results that we cannot imagine its continuing much further. Not only are the canonical traditions of the Mishnah and Talmuds considered part and parcel of Sinaitic revelation and therefore of equal standing, for all intents and purposes, with the Written Law. Not only do such modern authorities as R. David Tzvi Hoffmann consider the Oral Law to be contiguous with the Pentateuch for the purpose of applying the dicta of one to the other.[12] But, what is more, even the remarks and conclusions of later commentators are treated, within the literature of responsum and rabbinic ruling, as though they were revealed words, meriting the same sort of profound reading that the Mosaic Scriptures received in the *halakhah*. Sentences composed by eleventh- and even nineteenth-century commentators about issues specific to their day are held in such high esteem that they are frequently made to speak to situations that their authors could never have imagined. Their words and turns of phrase receive painstaking casuistic examination, without regard to how remote these sources may be from the problems at hand. R. Jonathan Eibschutz (Prague, 1695–1764) was outspoken in his support for such an approach,[13] and one can discern it even in the treatment of twentieth-century Rabbis in contemporary orthodoxy. In a sense, the process has come full circle. Oral Law was reconnected with Scriptures by means of classical rabbinic exegesis. The flourishing of rabbinic exegesis, in turn, stimulated interest in the concept of an independent Oral Law, as a theological corrective to the association of religious regulations with merely human authority. Now, however, this corrective has given rise to the preternaturalization of the Oral Law as a separately revealed Torah of Sinai. As a result, the religious world of Jewish orthodoxy no longer perceives the Oral Law as having arisen historically, and orthodox study of the extrabiblical sources has become deeply dissatisfying for anyone sensitive to the reality of history. The time may have come for the conclusions and rulings of human Rabbis to be lowered from the lofty status of divine revelation.

PART FIVE: TORAH RESTORED—
A THEOLOGICAL SOLUTION

One who believes in revelation and adheres to tradition would like to have faith, as the Rambam does, in a perfectly received revelation. The pious mind and the zealous soul want permission to consider the tradition received from the Rabbis to be the perfect expression of God's will to Moses on Mount Sinai. There is often little room in the religious heart to accept any uncertainty. Yet to live as a devoted Jew who is awake and responsible to history is to realize that the Torah of revelation has passed through the conduit of humankind and has been affected by the journey. Both written Law and oral tradition have passed through fire and water from the day of their arrival on this earth, and our sages of blessed memory were the first to admit that these legacies of revelation did not escape unscathed.

What then can we say of revelation, and what can we accept as the Torah of revelation? My answer is one admittedly governed by principles of necessity. To live as a Jew is to have a Law to live by. My solution is also one governed by fidelity to what we have inherited. For all its maculation, for all that it has passed through the vicissitudes of history, the Torah that we have inherited is the only testament we have to revelation as it was understood by our forebears. Knowing this instills in one a sense of reverence and unwillingness to tamper with what has already suffered so much at our hands. That said, there is also need for a critical perspective on the inherited tradition. Attention to the maculation and uncertainty inherent in our Torah, oral and written, and an appreciation of its history can be antidotes to intolerance: fostering deeper discernment of the many expressions of Torah, past and present.

Today, we do not share the infatuation of the sages with exegesis; we have inherited some of the skepticism and mistrust that eventually grew up around it. On the other hand, we are also unable to share the Rambam's faith in a divinely revealed Oral Torah, identical to rabbinic law; we are too aware of history and of how our rabbinic forebears have worked to shape the tradition. We must acknowledge that an Oral Law is indispensable and has been so since the Holy Scriptures were first translated into practice. At the same time, we cannot accept every statement made by every rabbi as authentic, revealed Oral Law.

Perhaps we may begin to build our conception of the Oral Law with the notion of indispensability—with those elements of the ex-

Cf. Quine [2]

trabiblical tradition that are absolutely necessary in order to live by the Scriptures. These are *basic definitions,* such as the identification of the etrog as *pri etz hadar* ("fruit of goodly trees," Leviticus 23:40) and the identification of the categories of work forbidden on the Sabbath. And there are *essential interpretations,* as for example the cases of divorce and levirate marriage. As we have already noted, we cannot be certain that the definitions and interpretations that we have inherited are identical to those that first accompanied the Scriptures as they were lived by our earliest Israelite ancestors. On the other hand, we can be certain that, from the outset, basic definitions and essential interpretations were needed at just these places. This need for an essential, extrascriptural tradition, combined with respect for the chain of tradition through which we inherit that tradition, can serve as the cornerstone of our conception of the essential Oral Law.

We must then distinguish this essential oral tradition from a genre of *extrascriptural teaching* that might be termed "pontification" or "opinion," and we must extend this distinction as far back in history as we can discern it. By contrast to the elementary definitions and explanations that are necessary to make the Scriptures practicable, this second genre of oral tradition arises not out of necessity but out of reflection upon the received law and upon the world to which it is applied. That reflection is inherently subjective and inseparable from the personalities and individual histories of the authorities who gave voice to it. To coin terms, one may say that I am arguing for a distinction between *da'at torah,* or "essential Oral Law," and *da'at chakhamim,* or "the legacy of subjective rabbinic opinion that has accrued to that Oral Law."

In addition to these two basic categories, we may discern the region of *gezerot* ("decrees") and *takkanot* ("remedial ordinances") that lies in nature and authority somewhere between the indispensable definitions and interpretations, on the one hand, and subjective opinions, on the other. It is well known that the sages instituted strictures to protect the essential Law and safeguard against its violation, and also that they occasionally innovated additional prescriptions and regulations in order to keep the Law viable and central in the life of the people. Such rabbinic contributions are also part of the Oral Law, and we may accept them without the skepticism and uncertainty that we reserve for *da'at chakhamim* because *gezerot* and *takkanot* present themselves truthfully for what they are, without aspiring to preternatural heights.

The medieval notion that virtually all rabbinic law was both revealed to Moses on Mount Sinai and also transmitted by him to the generations gave rise to an untenable theological generalization regarding the Oral Law: that every authoritative dictum found in a revered tome had the authority of revelation. By extension, even in our day, the words of noted sages of the Law—even when they are manifestly subjective and not based solely upon a weighing of the sources—are revered by their followers as if they emanated from the burning bush. An essential and healthy acknowledgment of any sage's humanity and fallibility is missing in the zeal of the pious, and that lack, which leads to intolerance and rigidity, is a legacy of the medieval elevation of the entire Oral Law to the level of revelation.

As a corrective, we may adopt a more critical and reserved attitude toward those elements of nonscriptural tradition, ancient and contemporary, that are not essential to the translation of the Scriptures into practice. For example, the Talmudic dictum that "women are light minded" (*Shabbat* 33b and parallels) need not be regarded as essential to the Law, even though it has undoubtedly had an impact upon the practice of the Law. Where *da'at chakhamim* is manifest, it is fitting to be open-minded and receptive to alternative possibilities. The greater the manifest involvement of subjective opinion in a given matter, the more we must acknowledge the human role in shaping the extrabiblical tradition and be appropriately humble and open-minded in our handling of the Law. By contrast, the more a given point within the Oral Law is necessary to the application of the Torah, the more we must be mindful of revelation and of the chain of tradition that links us to it.

Admittedly, the very discernment of *da'at torah* and *da'at chakhamim* and of their combinations and permutations within the Oral Law is itself an inescapably subjective matter. We cannot escape the involvement of human judgment in the reception of the Law that we want to call divine. Theologically, we may say that, ever since the Breaking of the Tablets, after the Sin of the Golden Calf, Torah has been an interplay between the divine and the human—an attempt to reconstitute the Torah of revelation. In that sense we may view the history of the Oral Torah in a positive and not only lachrymose manner. While acknowledging the brokenness that arises from human history—even in the Torah itself —we may also acknowledge the noble striving of our forebears, and ourselves, to recapture the Torah of Sinai.

NOTES

1. M. Kister, *Iyunim Beavot Derabbi Natan* (Jerusalem: Magnes Press, 1930): 220.

2. See the introduction to my commentary on Talmud *Eruvin, Mekorot Umasorot, Eruvin,* 91.

3. See R. Abraham's reference to the passage in Y. *Peah* 2:4 in his commentary on Exodus 24:12.

4. For other cases where R. Yehoshua b. Levi seems to oppose aggadic readings, see Y. *Shabbat* 16:1, Midrash *Tehilim* 22, and parallels. But for another perspective, see *Berakhot* 10a and *Baba Batra* 9b, end.

5. A version of this is cited by Hanania b. Achi R. Yehoshua in Y. *Shekalim* 49d.

6. Abramson, *Inyanot Besifrut Hageonim* (Jerusalem, 1974), 289–91.

7. For example, R. Eliezer in the Mishnah of *Yadaim* and R. Elazar b. Azariah in the *Sifra* on *Tzav.*

8. Mishnah *Yevamot* 8:3, *Ketubot* 3:9.

9. Lawrence Schiffman, *The Halacha at Qumran* (Studies in Judaism in Late Antiquity, No. 16) (Leiden: Brill, 1975): chap. 1.

10. *Tanchuma Kitisa* 34.

11. *Rule of the Community* 5:7–12.

12. See Hoffman's introduction to his commentary on Leviticus.

13. See Jonathan Eibschutz, *Kitzur Tokfa Kohen,* para. 124.

4

Epilogue:
Between Auschwitz and Sinai

David Weiss Halivni

Editor's Introduction

Peter Ochs

Composed as a reflection on the work of this book as a whole, this chapter returns to the themes of the prologue and first chapter. The liturgical message is that during the Shoah, Halivni prayed that God might rule over us again, reduce His distance from us, and thereby reduce humanity's capacity to practice its freedom in evil ways. Now Halivni prays the same prayer again, so that by reducing His distance from us He might enable us to see more clearly what He spoke to Moses and, thus, what our way of Torah should be. "We long," he says, "for the unadulterated word of God." The book has thus moved from historical and theological witness, to "depth" historiography, to plain-sense scholarship, then again to depth historiography and to prayer.

Halivni's prayer has implications for all four levels of his work. It is, of course, theological, and in this chapter Halivni traces out more fully his doctrine of God's distance and of our need to pray for His coming nearer. On a second level, his prayer corresponds to a scholarly claim about what the study of Torah means at times of God's greater nearness or distance: that, in times of God's distance, all we have are His previous words and our science. In times of God's distance, tradition is less reliable because it is more encumbered by merely human will. That does not leave us with science, alone, however. It also leaves us with established law, with a heightened desire to uncover the plain sense of the law for a given generation, and, finally, it also leaves us with a fervent prayer for God's return to renew us as in days of old, *l'chadesh yamenu k'kedem*.

If *Breaking the Tablets* belonged to the earlier phase of Halivni's writings, he might have concluded with a prayer but also with the disclaimer that the realm of prayer remains independent of the realm of scholarship. Now, however, his book concludes with some of the consequences of a third way of rabbinic scholarship. We see that the fact of our being stimulated to pray for God's nearness may itself be a sign of God's movement in that direction. If God is a touch nearer in prayer, then God is also a touch nearer in scholarship, which means that science, while dominant in our work, is not its exclusive source. Scientific judgments are framed by the context of prayer: not that there are some external words of prayer that any reader could use to extend the meaning of one's scholarship but that one situates an actual scientific discipline of scholarship in the practice of prayer.

For contemporary scholars, the analogy here is to what the historian of philosophy Pierre Hadot says about the ancient Stoics and other circles of classic Hellenistic philosophers: that their words of philosophy accompanied everyday lives of shared philosophic virtues and that what we see on the page is only the fruit of ascetic discipline and preparation. This is the sense we may now also have of the medieval theologian Anselm, that his great proofs of God's existence were not abstractions on the page but the fruit of meditations set into daily practices of prayer and ascetic and intellectual discipline. This is the sense we have always had of Maimonides, for whom what one did in scholarship did not make sense and did not work if it were not preceded by a discipline of mathematics and physics and halakhic behavior and prayer. Halivni does not say it in these terms, but I receive his last chapter as urging us to remember that, in order for rabbinic scholarship to discover what it discerns, it needs first to have prepared the pathways of mind, heart, and imagination, and these are prepared in some of the classical ways. Might we still say it is by mathematics, by logic, by prayer, by *mitsvot*, by good health, by textual science—and by observing where we stand in history and with whom and for what?

Epilogue: Between Auschwitz and Sinai

There were two major theological events in Jewish history, "Revelation" at Sinai and revelation at Auschwitz.[1] The former was a revelation of God's Presence, the latter a revelation of God's absence; the former indicated God's nearness to us, the latter God's distance. At Sinai, God appeared before Israel, addressed us and gave us instructions; at Auschwitz, God absented Himself from Israel, abandoned us, and handed us over to the enemy. In between these two periods, Israel's spiritual history took place, moving between God's embracing us at Sinai and God's withdrawing from us at Auschwitz, between divine intervention and divine abandonment, between our sense of connection and our sense of detachment. Every aspect of spiritual life is affected by this movement: the way we believe, the way we pray, the way we study His Torah, and the way we make ritual decisions. The way we view His connection to us affects our place and purpose in the universe. Our catechism and our beliefs are formed by it. Prayer is certainly affected by this movement, whether we concentrate on extolling God's greatness, lamenting His inaccessibility, or pleading that He shall not discard us, that "He should not take away the Holy Spirit from us," that He should continue to abide among us.

But how does this movement affect the study of Torah and the *halakhic* and theological decisions that issue from this study? The purpose of this chapter is to respond to this question by narrating the gradual erosion of God's Presence among us since Sinai so that, from the perspective of our relation to God, Auschwitz appears not as a sudden eclipse of God but as the ultimate outcome of a long process that began in the postbiblical period.

MIDRASH AS PARTNERSHIP WITH GOD

According to our history, the character of midrash changed through the rabbinic period, from the Rabbis' initial efforts to cleave to the living Torah even if it led them, at times, away from the plain sense, to their gradually diminished capacity to leave the plain sense, even for the sake of the living Torah. We attribute this decline to the gradual diminution of the Divine Presence. When He was close to the sages, he granted them some of His power to enact laws on their own. But when His presence diminished, the Rabbis had diminished access to this power and could be assured of God's Presence only within the Written Torah and its received meaning. From this time forward, any deviation from the literal meaning lacked Divine endorsement and acquired the status of merely human law. Human law acquires the status of Divine Law only when it is accompanied by the Divine Presence, and this accompaniment has diminished over time.

As I have argued on several occasions, Israel's greatest intimacy with God came at the time of Ezra (in the fifth century B.C.E.), after Israel ceased to worship idols and accepted the Torah as the sole guide of religious instruction. That is not to say that the impact of the Sinai Revelation was not felt during the first Temple period while the Jews were idol worshippers. Israel's turning to other gods was an act of defiance that could be made only in God's Presence. Emboldened by God's nearness at Sinai, Israel, as it were, exerted its independence and turned elsewhere. God chastised them but did not break off relations. By the time of Ezra, seven hundred years later, God's closeness was restored, albeit not to its state at Sinai. With that closeness, Ezra regained a considerable degree of the Sinaitic power of interpreting God's literal word. This means that Ezra could expound the Written Torah in ways that might have appeared, at the time, to diverge from the literal sense but that, in fact, merited Divine sanction, restoring the original meaning. "Midrash" at this time was not, therefore, a means of adding on to the text or deviating from it but a means of restoring its meaning. This was what we call "midrash at its maximum."

MIDRASH AT ITS MAXIMUM

It was an accepted axiom among the medieval Jewish philosophers that the Written Torah is by itself insufficient to serve as a guide for everyday behavior. It needs interpretation—midrash or elucidation— that would translate the general rulings of Torah into detailed laws applicable to practical life. For example, the biblical injunction "You shall not do any work on the Sabbath" does not tell us how we should otherwise behave on the Sabbath. To do so we need better and more clearly defined injunctions. These are indeed provided by the Rabbis, who, through the power of midrash, provided us a lengthy, all-inclusive system of practical laws that were integrated into the Divine Law. To display this integration, the Rabbis instituted blessings to be recited before one performs these laws; within the blessings, one thanks God for having commanded us to perform them.

How, then, did human interpretation become Divine Law? How did *midrashic* interpretation become Divine obligation? According to our narrative, midrash acquired divine sanction when God trusted in the Rabbis to be interpreters of the Written Law: to be His partners and complete what He left unrevealed. The Rabbis were authorized, as it were, in His stead, as if He Himself had commanded them, as if He hovered over them, assuring them of their capacity to join in the giving of Torah.

God put His trust in them even though He knows that, as human beings, they will make mistakes—and mistakes that even we can identify. God endorsed their activity nonetheless, including their apparent errors, as if this endorsement transformed their errant decisions into good ones. In order to provide such endorsement, He needed to reveal Himself anew to the *midrashic* legislators, and these new revelations could under certain circumstances annul what had been affirmed before. The tannaitic term for this annulment is *nitschuni banai*, "My children have overcome me."[2] It is as if God said, "I am now accepting their point of view; what was previously considered inappropriate may now be considered appropriate." These words indicate that, by virtue of the dispensation He granted them when He gave them the Torah to interpret despite their great tendency to err, God transformed the sages' errors into nonerrors.

This idea is expressed in Nachmanides' commentary on the biblical verse "You shall not deviate from their teaching right or left" (Deuteronomy 17:11). Noting that some Rabbis of the Talmud interpreted this verse to mean "(You have to obey them) even if they tell you of the right that it is left, or of the left that it is right," Nachmanides asks, "How can you obey a law that is mistaken?" His answer is that "God gave the Torah to the interpreters according to their understanding, (and we have to obey them) even when it looks like they are changing the right for the left or the left for the right." The force of Nachmanides' words is that, by empowering the sages to integrate their interpretations into Divine Law, God endorsed even their mistaken interpretations. When, however, the sages ceased receiving direct divine communication, then their endorsement ceased as well, and their mistaken rulings could no longer be treated as valid.

The sages' powers were taken away only gradually. God's closeness gradually diminished, and, without that closeness, their errant legislations lost Divine sanction. We may, in fact, distinguish three general phases of closeness. In the time of Ezra, interpretation was at its early stage, and human partnership was indispensable for rendering the Divine Law operational in Israel's everyday life. This phase of closeness continued through the first generation of Rabbis (the "Pairs," *zugot*) lending them the power on occasion to deviate from the literal meaning of the text. The next generations of Rabbis, the *tannaitic* authors of the Mishnah, had no such power and only readings that complied with the *peshat* were acceptable. On occasion the Tannaim appealed to direct divine intervention (*bat kol*) to adjudicate their decisions. This *bat kol* did not, however, lend them right to deviate from the *peshat* but only to decide controversies or at times to accept a human decision over a Divine decision (which is the case of *nitschuni banai*, where God first decided in favor of Rabbi Eliezer and then, conceding to His "children," endorsed the view of Rabbi Eliezer's opponent, Rabbi Joshua. After this endorsement, R. Eliezer's view was prohibited). The period of the Amoraim, the Rabbis that followed the Tannaim, was marked by a diminished sense of God's presence and, thus, diminished tolerance for changes in the Divine Law and deviations from the literal meaning of the Bible. The Amoraim did not appeal to a *bat kol* to decide halakhah but made their decisions on the basis of consensus, which became binding on future generations as well. To achieve consensus, they appealed to logical arguments grounded in plausible exegeses of the texts before them. On occasion, however, they too argued that even contradictory views could each be valid, that *elu v'elu*, "both are the words of the living God."

Divine intervention in any form was rare after the time of the *Amoraim*, after the Talmud was more or less concluded. On occasion, one comes across a book like that of Rabbi Yaakov Shoel Shaloth min Hasomaim—one of the *Tosafists*, active around the thirteenth century—in which R. Yaakov addresses questions to God and God answers him in a dream.[3] Despite their claims, however, the authors of such books did not carry any greater authority than most other decisors of their rank. Since the time of the Amoraim, in other words, God's presence was increasing diminished, and He no longer intervened directly in the process of forming halakhah.

A HISTORY OF THE DIMINISHED PARTNERSHIP

Having introduced our understanding of midrash as partnership with God, we may now examine more detailed illustrations of how God's diminishing presence reduced the Rabbis' role in divine legislation. A number of major rabbinic laws are based on interpretations that deviate from the literal meaning of the text. The two most prominent examples are interpretations of "an eye for an eye" and of the Levirate marriage. According to the literal sense, Exodus 21:23 refers to a physical eye, and the Rabbis bring unconvincing proofs that the text refers to monetary compensation equivalent to the use of an eye. Nonetheless, the Rabbis accept the latter reading, as demonstrated in the case of Rabbi Eliezer (*Baba Kamma* 84a). Against the majority, Rabbi Eliezer argued for the plain sense, but the Talmud rejected his opinion as impossible. As for the levirate marriage, the plain sense of Deuteronomy 25:6 is clear: that the first born child of the levirate union "shall succeed in the name of his brother that is dead" and, thus, that the first born child will be considered the offspring of the deceased. This meaning is also implied by the way the case of Onan is worded: "And Onan knew that the seed would not be his" (Genesis 38:9). The Rabbis could not, however, accept the notion that someone other than the physical father would be considered the real father of the next born child. They therefore interpreted the text to mean that the oldest brother, the one who was born first, will perform the levirate marriage, an interpretation that flagrantly overturns the plain sense of the text, as the Rabbis of the Talmud themselves acknowledged (*Yevamoth* 24a). These nonliteral interpretations of both Exodus 21:23 and Deuteronomy 25:6 seem to have been fully accepted during the early period of the Tannaim, who disagreed only in minor details of application. This is because they considered these interpretations divinely ordained, reflecting much older laws from the time of Ezra and the High Synod.[4]

In the period of the Tannaim, however, God's presence was already diminished, so that the Tannaim lost the power of their predecessors to receive divine sanction for most of their nonliteral readings. However, while the sages no longer received direct divine endorsement for their interpretations, a Divine Voice (*bat kol*) would appear to them on occasion to resolve controversies on matters of religious law. In cases of conflict between the Hillelites and the Shammaites, for example, God instructed them to follow the rulings of the Hillelites. As illustrated in the famous cases of the Oven of Achnai, God was even prepared to change His mind. When Rabbi Eliezer ruled against the majority opinion, the Divine Voice first instructed the Rabbis to follow Rabbi Eliezer. In the face of Rabbi Joshua's obstinate defense of the majority, however, God relented and sanctioned the majority opinion. We might note that, while the first *bat kol* was delivered directly to the people—albeit on behalf of Rabbi Eliezer's solicitation—God's acquiescence to the majority opinion was not delivered directly. It came in response to an inquiry by Rabbi Nathan to Elijah the Prophet: "What did God do at that time [when Rabbi Joshua refused to accept the Divine Voice on the ground "that the Torah is not in Heaven and religious decisions are not made there any more]"? Elijah the Prophet answered, "God smiled and said 'My children overcame me, my children overcame me.'" Perhaps out of modesty, God's change of mind was not directly announced.

The Divine Presence diminished even further after the *tannaitic* period, during the time of the Amoraim, when the sages were no longer privileged to receive even the *bat kol* and even in cases of controversy. Divine intervention ceased, in other words, as if God were not there to intervene. As previously mentioned, however, this applied only to matters of law; outside of the halakhah, the Rabbis continued to draw on the flow of divine guidance. In one instance, in fact, divine influence flowed the other way, and aggadah influenced the halakhah. The Talmud (*Baba Metsia* 86a) relates that a controversy over matters of ritual purity once broke out between God Almighty and the Heavenly Academy. Heaven then turned to the Amora, Rabbi Raba, the son of Nachman, to decide the controversy (Raba, who lived during the second half of the fourth century, was a great expert in laws of ritual purity). Raba agreed with the Divine opinion and declared it pure. Yet, seven hundred years later, Maimonides, in his *Mishnah Torah*, codified as law the opinion of the Heavenly Academy, which is also the opinion of the Mishnah that preceded Raba by at least two hundred years. Maimonides may have viewed the story of Raba as nonlegal literature, or aggadah, and therefore as nonbinding. Overall, the development of the aggadic literature is nonlinear, zigzagging back and forth throughout history, without any discernible continuity of development. The history of God's diminishing presence between Sinai and Auschwitz is thus exclusively a history of God's diminishing participation in the process of Jewish law.

While the Amoraim lacked divine authorization to interpret against the literal meaning of the Bible and lacked a Divine Voice to decide halakhic controversies, they still retained a degree of divine endorsement through the convention of "consensus." When a legal controversy remains unresolved in the Talmud, a decisor may, on the basis of any new arguments, choose to follow either side. If, however, the Talmud has arrived at a consensus, its decision becomes binding and cannot be overridden. Though deprived of direct Divine Presence, the Talmud retains its religious authority by virtue of the biblical commandment to obey the legislators (Deuteronomy 17:11). In the introduction to his *Mishnah Torah*, Maimonides attributes the power of the Talmud to its universal acceptance among the different Jewish communities. According to the traditional saying, "If it is written in the Talmud, it is undisputable." Whether the Talmud always had this authority or acquired it only centuries later, its unparalleled degree of acceptance for more than a millennium bestowed on it a quality of Divine endorsement.

After the Talmudic period, God's presence has been minimal in the process of legal decision making: too minimal to help decide halakhic controversies or to endorse new legal decisions. There have been attempts to attribute a degree of extra, albeit nonsupernatural, power to the Gaonim—the scholars that followed the Talmud—and thus render their opinions obligatory. Such attempts were, however, challenged by Rabbi Asher (the thirteenth-century commentator, the "Rosh," in his commentary on Tractate *Sanhedrin* 4:6) on the grounds that the Talmud remains the superauthority, so that in case of any conflict between the Talmud and the opinion of any Gaon, one should follow the Talmud. While he assumes that no one would disagree with a Gaon on the basis of logic alone, without proof from the Talmud, the Rosh also argues in principle that, if he feels strongly about the logic of his own reasoning, then one may oppose a Gaon's opinion on logical grounds alone.

The *Shulchan Arukh* (a sixteenth-century code of law) has comparable status. On the one hand, there are those who attribute a Divine quality to the *Shulchan Arukh* and regard deviations from it with suspicion. In many circles, there is in fact a great hesitancy to deviate from its rulings, as if they had a Divine imprimatur, as if the Divine Presence accompanied its composition. Rabbi Jonathan of Eibsitz (nineteenth-century scholar, in his introduction to *Kitzur Tokfa Kohen*) sees a Divine quality inherent in the *Shulchan Arukh* in the fact that we seek guidance from it for occurrences that emerged after its time. That could only be, he reasons, if its authors had a tinge of prophecy, sensing—even if unconsciously—what will take place in the future. On the other hand, I take it for granted that the scholars who frequently disagree with the *Shulchan Arukh*—such as the *Sach* (Rabbi Shabti Katz, seventeenth-century scholar) and the *Pri Chadash* (eighteenth century)—did not consider it to possess Divine qualities. They would not have quarreled with a divinely endorsed opinion. Laws that the tradition considers divine are laws that were pronounced in God's presence at a time when that presence was strong. From the time of Ezra and the High Synod to the time of Auschwitz, God's presence has steadily declined and, with it, God's sanction for new law.

In short, the horrendous Divine abandonment that took place during the years of the Shoah marked the nadir of a long, gradual process that may have already begun with the Golden Calf. To paraphrase a Talmudic saying; "If the Tablets were not broken, the Torah would not have been forgotten." "If they would not have abandoned God by worshipping the Golden Calf, God would not have abandoned us in the years to follow." But He did abandon us, and His absence has affected all aspects of Jewish spiritual life, including the way we interpret the Torah. God's presence among us has given us license on occasion to deviate from the *peshat*, or the plain meaning of the text, corresponding to the strict, intended meaning sought after in recent years by critical or scientific scholars of the text. When God was among us, the text was subordinated to His Will, which manifested itself at times in interpretations that deviated from the *peshat* or plain sense. But now, we have only the text itself, and we are guided by its plain sense alone.

We who live in the post-Auschwitz era hope and have every reason to believe that the pendulum has swung back and that God is getting closer to us.[5] Yet, as far as the study *of* halakhah is concerned, our task remains the same, to perfect the literal meaning. We cannot override the text.

IN CONCLUSION: PRAYER AFTER THE SHOAH

Prayer, like any other religious behavior, does not ask for change, even in the face of the terrible tragedy that eclipsed our generation; religiously we act as if we are still under the mantle of the Revelation at Sinai. Nevertheless, personal emphasis and intention, *kavanah*, is an indispensable accompaniment of prayer, and this accompaniment ought to be different today than in the past, prior to Auschwitz.

In the past we extolled the glory of God's power over our limited powers; in the words of the daily morning prayer, "Thine, o Lord, is the greatness, and the power, the glory and the victory and the majesty" (from I Chronicles 20:10–13). Today, however, adding emphasis and *kavanah* to this prayer would further extend the distance between God and us, increasing our alienation in the universe. Today, it is more suitable for us to add emphasis and *kavanah* to the prayer of *Modim*, recited three times a day: "We *acknowledge* (that is the right translation) that You are the strength of our own life and our saving shield. In every generation we will thank You and recount Your graces for our lives that are in Your charge, for our souls that are in Your care." This prayer emphasizes God's closeness to us, an assurance that His alienation will not last forever.

For the sake of our theology today, we need prayers like the one we recite on Rosh Hashanah: "Our God and God of our fathers, reign in Your glory over the whole universe, and be exalted above the whole earth . . . , so that whatever has been made may know that You made it; so that whatever has been created may understand that You created it; and so that whatever has breath in its nostrils may say, 'The Lord God of Israel is King and has dominion over all.'"

Only a prayer that pleads that God will retake the reign He forfeited for the sake of granting free will to sinful human creatures; only a prayer that pleads for the curtailment of God's *tsimtsum*, the withdrawal by means of which He was able to create a finite and corruptable world; only a prayer that acknowledges that God's purpose of creation is for us to worship Him, to obey Him, to be close to Him; only prayers like these may heal the terrible wound that recent history has inflicted on us and shorten the distance between the two major events in Jewish history, Sinai and Auschwitz. Amen.

NOTES

1. The first term for revelation is capitalized to indicate that we are dealing with two very different meanings of "revelation."

2. *Baba Metsia* 59 a–b.

3. And he was not the only one to do so, as is pointed out in great detail by the editor of this work, R. R. Margolioth (*Mosad Harav Kook*, Jerusalem, 1953).

4. The source of these laws could not be earlier than Ezra since, from the time of the Golden Calf up to the time of Ezra, the Jews were idol worshippers and did not consider the Torah the source of their religious instruction, certainly not the exclusive source. At the time of Ezra and the High Synod, interpretation was divinely sanctioned even when it seemed to be against the text. God's presence was so strong in that period that God shared, as it were, in the sages' deliberations, lending their conclusions divine sanction if not outright authorship.

5. Some interpret the establishment of the State of Israel as a sign of this.

Contemporary Works Cited

TEXTS BY DAVID WEISS HALIVNI

Mekorot Umasorot ("Sources and Traditions") (Jerusalem: 1968–):
  Seder Nashim (Tel-Aviv: 1968)
  Yoma-Chagigah (Jerusalem: 1974)
  Shabbat (Jerusalem: 1982)
  'Eruvin-Pesachim (Jerusalem: 1982)
  Baba Kama (Jerusalem: 1993)
  Baba Metsia (Jerusalem: 2003)
  Baba Batra (Jerusalem: 2007)
Midrash, Mishna and Gemara (Cambridge, MA, and London: Harvard University
  Press, 1986)
Peshat and Derash: Plain and Applied Meaning in Rabbinic Exegesis (Oxford: Oxford
  University Press, 1991).
Revelation Restored: Divine Writ and Critical Response (Boulder, CO: Westview
  Press, 1997).
The Book and the Sword: A Life of Learning in the Shadow of Destruction (New
  York: Farrar, Straus and Giroux, 1996; Boulder, CO: Westview Press: 1998).
Iyunim Behithavot Hatalmud ("*Reflections on the Formation of the Talmud*")
  (Jerusalem: Magnes Press, 2008).

CONTEMPORARY TEXTS

Berkowitz, Eliezer. *Faith after the Holocaust*. New York: Ktav, 1973.

———. *With God in Hell*. New York: Sanhedrin Press, 1979.

Boyarin, Daniel. *Intertextuality and the Reading of* Midrash. Bloomington: Indiana University Press, 1990.

Chartum, Rabbi Menachem Emmanuel, "Reflections on the Shoah," *Deot* 18 (Heb.) (winter 1961): 28–37.

Fackenheim, Emil. *The Jewish Return to History: Reflections in the Age of Auschwitz and a New Jerusalem*. New York: Schocken, 1978.

Faur, Jose. *Golden Doves with Silver Dots*. Tampa: University of South Florida, 2000 [orig. 1984].

Fishbane, Michael. *Biblical Interpretation in Ancient Israel*. Oxford: Oxford University Press, 1985.

Fraade, Steven. *From Tradition to Commentary: Torah and Its Interpretation in the Midrash Sifre to Deuteronomy*. Albany: State University of New York Press, 1991.

Frei, Hans. *The Eclipse of Biblical Narrative: A Study in Eighteenth and Nineteenth Century Hermeneutics*. New Haven, CT: Yale University Press, 1980.

Greenberg, Gershon. "Between Holocaust and Redemption: Silence, Cognition, and Eclipse" and "Ultra-Orthodox Jewish Throught about the Holocaust since World War II, in *The Impact of the Holocaust on Jewish Theology*, ed. Steven T. Katz. New York: New York University Press, 2005, 110–31, 132–60.

Greenberg, Irving. "Cloud of Smoke, Pillar of Fire," in *Auschwitz: Beginning of a New Era?*, ed. Eva Fleischer. New York: Ktav, 1977.

Greenberg, Moshe. "The Vision of Jerusalem in Ezekiel 8–11: A Holistic Interpretation," in *The Divine Helmsman, Studies on God's Control of Human Events, Presented to Lou. H. Silberman*, ed. J. L. Crenshaw and S. Sandmel. New York: KTAV, 1980, 143–63.

Gutterman, Bella, and Naomi Morgenstern, ed. *The Wolfsberg Machzor 5705 Wolfsberg Labor Camp Germany 1944*. Jerusalem: Yad Yashem, 2002.

Handelman, Susan. *The Slayers of Moses*. Albany: State University of New York Press, 1982.

Jonas, Hans. "The Concept of God after Auschwitz," in *Out of the Whirlwind*, ed. A. H. Friedlander. Garden City, NY: Doubleday, 1968, 465–76.

Joseph, Howard. "Some Jewish Theological Reflections on the Holocaust," in *Truth and Compassion: Essays on Judaism and Religion in Memory of Rabbi Dr. Solomon Frank*, ed. Howard Joseph, Jack M. Lightstone, and Michael Oppenheimer. Waterloo, Ont.: Published for the Canadian Corp. for Studies in Religion by Wilfrid Laurier University Press, 1983, 191–99.

Kadushin, Max. *The Rabbinic Mind*. New York: Bloch, 1972 [orig. 1952].

Kaplan, Lawrence. "Rabbi Isaac Hutner's 'Daat Torah Perspective' on the Holocaust: A Critical Analysis." *Tradition* Vol. 18 No. 3 (Fall 1980): 235–48.

Katz, Steven. "The Uniqueness of the Holocaust: The Historical Dimension," in *Is the Holocaust Unique?*, ed. Allen S. Rosenbaum. Boulder, CO: Westview Press, 1978, 19–37.

Kister, M. *Iyunim Beavot Derabbi Natan*. Jerusalem: Magnes Press, 1930.

Lamm, Norman. "The Face of God: Thoughts on the Holocaust," an address delivered to students of Yeshivah College, May 6, 1986.

Maza, B. *With Fury Poured Out: A Torah Perspective on the Holocaust*. Hoboken, NJ: Ktav, 1986.

Ochs, Peter. "Introduction to David Weiss Halivni's 'Prayer in the Shoah,'" in *Judaism* 199, vol. 50, no. 3 (summer 2001): 259–67.

——. "Talmudic Scholarship as Textual Reasoning: Halivni's Pragmatic Historiography," in *Textual Reasonings: Jewish Philosophy and Text Study at the End of the Twentieth Century*, ed. P. Ochs and N. Levene. Grand Rapids, MI: Eerdmans, 2003, 120–43.

Roskies, David. *The Literature of Destruction: Jewish Responses to Catastrophe*. Philadelphia: Jewish Publication Society, 1992.

Ross, Tamar. *Expanding the Palace of Torah: Orthodoxy and Feminism*. Boston: Brandeis University Press, 2004.

Sacks, Jonathan. "The Holocaust in Jewish Ideology," *Holocaust and Genocide Studies* 1988 3(4): 371–81.

Schiffman, Lawrence. *Halacha at Qumran*. Leiden: Brill, 1975.

Schweid, Eliezer. "The Struggles of Orthodox Judaism with the Shoah" (Heb.) (Machanayim: Kislev, 5755): 13–18.

Sherbok, Dan Cohn. *Holocaust Theology*. London: Lamp Press, 1989.

Taichtal, Rabbi Y. S. *A Happy Mother of Children* (Heb.) (Jerusalem, 5743).

Ta-Shma, Israel M., "Bible Criticism in Early Medieval Franco-Germany" (Heb.), in *The Bible in the Light of Its Interpreters*, Sarah Kamin Memorial Book, ed. Sarah Japhet. Jerusalem: Magnes Press, 1994.

Teitelbaum, Joel. (Satmar Rebbe), *Vayoel Moshe* (Heb.) (New York, 1959).

——. "On Redemption and Ruth 4:7" (Heb.) (New York, 1967).

Wiesel, Eliezer. "Prayer and the Modern Person," in *Jewish Prayer: Continuity and Innovation*, ed. Gabriel Chaim Cohen. Ramat Gan: The Institute for Judaism and Contemporary Thought, 1978, 13–26.

Index of Biblical and Rabbinic Sources

BIBLICAL SOURCES

Bible

Genesis	25:22	54
	38:9	111
	43:30	41
Exodus	21:23	111
	23:5	90
	24:12	101
Leviticus	11:4–6	56–57
	18:28	18
	20:22	18
	23:40	99
	26	18, 23, 40
	26:33	23
	26:38	23
	26:44	17, 39
Deuteronomy	5:26	35
	9:10	87
	13:3	40
	14	56
	14:7	56

	15:2	63
	17:11	109, 113
	25:5	90
	25:6	111
	28	18
	31:17–18	32
Joshua	7:20	41
2 Kings	22–23	90, 91
Isaiah	59:2	32
	56:7	32, 34
	56:4	35
Jeremiah	9:15	20
	10:24	19, 24
	13:14	20
	14:12	20
	30:11	19, 20, 24
	39:6–7	29
	40:12	30
	42:44	21
	42:20	21
	44:12–14	21
	44:14	22
	44:18	21
	44:23	21
	46:28–29	19, 22
Ezekiel	5:13	21
	7	21
	29:17	40
Psalms	25:14	85
	83	40
	93:16	32
	118:18	40
Proverbs	10:7	28
Lamentations	4:4	28
Ecclesiastes	7:13	55
	7:20	35
Ezra	7:10	54

Nehemiah	8:1–8	xxvi
	9:6	22
	9:36	22
	9:27	22
	9:28	22
	9:17	23
	9:31	23
1 Chronicles	20:10–13	115
2 Chronicles	34	90, 91
	35:13	92

Dead Sea Scrolls

Rule of The Community (1QS)	5:7–12.	93–94, 101
Seder Olam	ch. 26 (near end)	22, 40

CLASSICAL RABBINIC LITERATURE

Mishnah

Yoma	3:11	28
Sota	3:3	41
Gittin	4:3	58, 63
Shabbat	16:1	100
Succah	5:2	58
Avot	1:1	62
Sheviit	10:3	63
Yadaim		101
	4:3	84
Baba Kama	5:7	94
Yevamot	8:3	101
Ketubot	3:9	101

Tosefta   95

Sanhedrin	4:3	40
Hallah	1:9	55
Yevamot	6:8	63

Babylonian Talmud

Berakhot	5a	86
	7a	34
	10a	21, 32, 33, 41, 101
Hullin	5a	22
Hagigah	13a	21
Temura	16a	63
	21a	63
Yevamot	24a	111
Baba Kama	38b	25
	54b	95
	84a	111
Baba Metsi'a	86a	63, 112, 116
Baba Batra	9b	101
	52b	41
Pesachim	118a	25
Sanhedrin	21a	53, 113
Yoma	85b–86a	40
	28b	81
Shabbat	55a	25
	55b	26
	63a	60
	31a	81–82, 85
	33b	100
Niddah	72b	84
Megillah	19b	87
Betsah	5b	29
Eruvin	54a	vi, 59, 88
Ketubot	42b	60
Gittin	55a	58

Talmud Yerushalmi

Peah	2:4	87, 88, 101
Shabbat	16:1	101
Shekalim	49d	101

Targumim

Targum Yonatan to Jer. 10, 30	20
Targum Onkelos to Gen 43:30	41

Rabbbinic Liturgy (classical and medieval sources)

Birkhat Hamazon ("Grace after Meals") 41
Rosh Hashanah Machzor, Amidah 15, 17, 36, 105, 115
Amidah (Sabbath, Holiday, Daily) 36
Aleinu (Daily) 36, 42
Blessings (Daily Morning) 115

Midrash Collections

Avot de Rabbi Natan, nuscha bet 82
Mekhilta Pischa (Mishpatim) 20 63
    Shirata 6 23–24
Sifra Shemini 4:5 55–57
    Bechukotai 82–85, 90
    Behar 83
    Tzav 101
    Deuteronomy 14:56 57–58, 63
Sifre Deuteronomy §113 63
    §213 63
    §339 41
    §351 85
Midrash Lamentations 2:6 32
Midrash Tehillim on Psalm 78:38 40
    22 101
Midrash Shir Hashirim Rabba 5:12 89
Tanhuma Kitisa 34 101

Josephus:

Antiquities 10.9.7 22

POST-TALMUDIC RABBINIC LITERATURE

R. Saadya Gaon (Saadya ben Joseph, 9th cent.). 41
    Ginzei Kedem II 89
R. Shrira Gaon: (10th cent.):
    On *Baba Metsi'a* 86a: 61, 63
R. Chananel ben Chushiel ("Rabbenu Chananel," 10–11th cent.
    Gaon): 81
R. Nissim Ben Jacob (Nissim Gaon, 10–11th cent.): 91

R. Solomon b. Isaac (Shlomo Yitzhaqi, "Rashi," 11th cent. commentator):

    On Jer. 30   20
    On Lev. 26   24
    Midrash Tehilim on Psalm 78:38   40
    On Sifra Behar   83

Ibn Ezra, Abraham ben Meir (11–12th cent.):
    on Lev 26:25   24

R. Yehudah Halevi (Judah ben Samuel Halevi, 11–12th cent.):
    Kuzari   78, 95, 96

R. Judah ben Barzillai of Barcelona (12th cent.):
    on the Sefer Yetzirah)   41

Rabbi Yaakov Shoel Shaloth min Hasomaim
    (12th cent.)   111, 116

Tosafot on B. Talmud:
    Menachot 58b63
    Shabbat 55a   41

R. Abraham ben David of Posquières ("The Rabad," 12th cent. Tosafist):
    on the Sifra   55, 57, 63

Joseph ben Isaac Bekhor Shor (12th cent. Tosafist)   62

R. David Kimchi ("Radak," 12–13th cent):
    On Jer. 10:24   19–20

R. Menahem Hameiri, Bet Habechira (13th cent.):
    on *Shabbat* 55b   25, 26

R. Asher ("The Rosh"): on Sanhedrin 4:6   113–14

R. Moses b. Jacob of Coucy (13th cent. Tosafist)
    Sefer Mitzvot Gadol (SMaG)   79–80, 96

Chaim Vital (16th cent. Kab.): Etz Chayim   41

Rabbi Joseph Karo (16th cent.): on Jeremiah 44:14
    (citing *Seder Olam*)   22

R. Eliyahu Mizrachi (16th cent.):
    commentary on Rashi on Lev 26   24, 40

R. Moses ben Maimon
    ("Rambam," Maimonides, 12th cent):
    27, 49, 62, 80, 82, 87, 89, 96, 98, 106
    Guide of the Perplexed, 1–13 III–17
        25–26
    Commentary on Mishnah Sota   41
    Mishnah Torah (Intro.)   91, 113
    On Sifra: Behar   83
    Introduction to the Mishnah   77–78

R. Moshe ben Nahman Gerondi ("Ramban," Nachmanides,
    12–13th cent.) On Deut. 17:11   109–10

R. Abraham ben Rambam (13th cent.):
        on *Megillah* 19b   87
        on *Y. Peah* 2:4   88, 101
R. Bezalel Ashkenzi (15th cent.): Shita Mekubeset
        on *Baba Batra* 52b   41
Don Isaac Abravanel (Isaac ben Judah Abravanel, 15th cent.):
        On Joshua 7:20.   41
R. Eliahu Mizrachi ("The Ram," 15–16th cent.):
        On Lev. 26   40
R. Joseph (Yosef) Karo (15–16th cent.):
        Shulchan Arukh   114
R. Aharon ben Avraham ibn Chayim (16th–17th cent.):
        Korban Aharon (commentary
        on the Sifra)   55, 57, 63, 95
R. Shabti Katz (the "Sach," 17th cent.):   114
R. Eliyahu of Vilna ("The Vilna Goan," 18th cent.)   55, 63
R. Chizkiya ben David DiSilo (17th cent.):
        Pri Chadash   14
R. Moses ben Samuel Sofer ("Hatam Sofer," 18–19th cent.)
  Novellae on BT. *Ketubot*   60, 63
R. Meir Leibush ben Yechiel Michel ("Malbim,"19th cent.):
        on Sifra   55, 56, 63
R. Israel Salanter (19th cent.): Sefer Tevunah No. 1   60, 63
R. Jonathan of Eibsitz (19th cent.):
        Kitzur Tokfa Kohen   97, 114
R. David Tzvi Hoffmann (19–20th cent.):   97

General Index

academic, academy, xiv–xxix, 6–7, 9–10, 46–50, 62, 71

acharei rabim lehatot ("to go according to the majority opinion of a given generation"), 49

Aggadah, aggadic literature, 11–12, 26, 34, 88, 101, 112–13

Aleinu, 36, 41, 58, 105

Amidah. *See* prayer

Amoraim, Amoraic, xi, xxi, 29, 41, 54, 59–62, 67–71, 81–89, 95–97, 108–13

Anselm, 106

Auschwitz. *See* concentration camps

Babylonians, 21–22, 29–30, 75, 90

Baumgarten, Murray, xxix, 13, 40

b'hadi kivshi d'rachmana lamah lakh ("Why do you concern yourself with the secrets of the Merciful One?"), 32

Bible, xiv, xvi, xxii, xxvi, 7, 10–11, 23, 48, 53, 92, 110, 113. *See also* Torah, Scripture

canonization, 16, 68, 74, 86, 92, 97

chasurei mechsera ("[The Mishnah] must have omitted a phrase"), 60

Chate'u yisrael. See Sins of Israel

concentration camps: Auschwitz, v, x–xii, xviii–xxi, xxvi–xxvii, 4–5, 11, 13, 28, 30–31, 38–39, 45, 107–8, 113–16; Maidenek, 28; Wolfsberg, 3–4, 15, 37, 40

controversies, rabbinic argument, debate (*shakla v'taria*). *See* Halakhah

creation, xviii, xx, 6, 22, 33–34, 58, 115

Da'at torah and *da'at chakhamim,* 99–100

Destruction, 5, 6, 9–14, 17–31, 38, 54, 92. *See also* L'khalotam; Temple

Ehud hamekorot ("unity of the sources"), 2–10

Evil, xxii, 9, 20, 22, 26, 27–37, 94, 105

exile, xxvi, 18, 21–24, 30, 75, 89–92
extrabiblical tradition, extrascriptural
    teaching, 76, 92–93, 96–100
Ezra, xxvii, 11, 54, 59, 68, 90, 108,
    110, 112, 114, 116

Fishbane, Michael, 14
forced interpretations (*dochok*),
    covering over, smooth reading,
    xxiv, xix, xxvii, 12, 47–51, 59–62,
    67, 70
Fraade, Steven, xv, xxix, 51, 72
Free Will (of humanity, granted by
    God), 33–36, 45, 59, 105, 115
Frei, Hans, xxiii

Geonim (general references), 7, 69,
    71, 113–14
Gemara, xiv, xvi, xxii, 25–26, 34, 40,
    49, 60, 69–70, 86–87, 95
God: Bat Kol (Divine voice):
    110–12; chastisements by,
    19–20, 108; distance of ("near-
    abence," "absence,"), x–xi,
    xvii–xviii, xxi, 12, 45–48, 67–68,
    107–16; *Hamakom* ("the Place,"
    No place is empty of Him), 33;
    Hiding of Face (*hester panim*), 32,
    38; Holy One, 19–20, 32–36, 39;
    Mercy of, Merciful One, 1–22,
    1–27, 29, 32, 34–35, 37;
    nearness of (*see* presence of);
    power of, 34–35, 47, 108, 115;
    prayer by, 34–35; presence or
    nearness of, x–xi, xvii–xix, 9, 11,
    33, 45, 48–49, 105–16;
    sovereignty, kingship or rule of
    (*malkhut*), God as King (*see*
    Melokh); *Tsimtsum* (Divine
    contraction), 9–10, 12, 33–36,
    38, 45, 115; will of: 19–26, 31,
    33–34, 36–39, 45, 50, 68, 71, 76,
    98, 114 (*see also* free will); word

of, xvii, xix, xxi, 37, 53, 59, 62,
    69, 78, 87, 105, 108–10
Great Assembly, High Synod,
    Knesset Hagadol, 49, 112, 114,
    116
Greenberg, Gershon, xxviii
Greenberg, Irving, 39

Hadot, Pierre, 106
halakha lemoshe misinai ("Oral Law
    passed down from Sinai"), xxiv,
    54, 67, 68, 71, 84–85, 88
halakha, legal literature, legislation,
    xiv, xviii–xxvi, 8, 11, 20, 29, 36,
    41, 49–50, 53–54, 59, 62,
    67–100, 109–13, 115; halakhic
    debate, legal controversies (legal
    "give-and-take," *shakla v'taria*),
    xxiii, 4, 25–27, 57, 61, 40, 69,
    78, 85 92, 96, 110–13;
    preternaturalization of (tendency
    to elevate rabbinic law to the
    status of divine revelation),
    96–97, 99
Hillel, 58, 63, 81–82, 112
Hirsch, Samson Raphael, xiv

idolatry, xvii, 21–22, 54, 91, 108,
    116
imagination, xiii, xxiv–xxv, 4–5, 9–13,
    30, 69, 84, 87, 90–91, 97, 106
interpretation. *See* Torah
Imo anochi b'tsara ("I am with him
    [Israel] in suffering," Psalm
    93:16), 32
Israel (people of), 11, 13, 17, 54;
    God's promise to or Covenant
    with, 17–37, 45, 54, 71, 81–100,
    107–16; *Klal yisrael* ("all Israel"),
    8, 23, 24, 26; Land of, 29, 38;
    "Sins of Israel" (*chate'u yisrael*)
    (*see* sins); State of, 116; suffering
    or exile of (*see* exile; suffering)

Joshua, 62, 78
Josiah, 54, 91
Judah Hanasi, Yehudah Hanasi, 74–75, 85–88, 96

Kabbalah, Lurianic. *See* Luria
Karaites, 78, 96–97
Katz, Steve, xxviii, 38
Kohanim, Levi'im, 28–29

Levinas, Emmanuel, xxix
levirate marriage, 99, 111
L'drosh ("to interpret"). *See* Midrash; Torah
L'khalotam ("to annihilate them"), 17–31, 40, 41
logic. *See* reasoning
Luria, R. Isaac, Lurianic Kabbalah, 9–12, 33, 41, 55, 57–59

Machzor. *See* prayer
maculate, maculation. *See pagam*
Maidenek. *See* concentration camps
Maimonides ("Rambam"), 25–27, 41, 49, 62, 77–78, 80, 82–83, 87, 89, 91, 96, 98, 106, 113
martyrs, 10, 22, 27
Mekorot Umasorot (book by Halivni), xiii, xv, xix, 6, 12, 48, 60, 63, 67, 69–72, 101
Mekorot ("sources"), *masorot* ("traditions"), xiii, xix, xii–xxviii, 6–14, 16, 21, 28, 29, 30, 32–33, 37, 46–51, 54, 61, 68–71, 74–100, 114
Midrash (rabbinic interpretation of scripture): xi, xxiii–xxix, 8–28, 32–33, 35, 40–41, 54–63, 68–72, 73–101, 108–13; "double-dialogue" (relation between text and commentators acc. to Bakhtin and Fraade), 72; maximal distance of God in midrash, xvii–xxi, 12,

45–48, 67–8, 105, 107–16; minimal distance of God in midrash, 33–34, 48, 105, 107–16; human freedom and midrash, 9–10, 45; maximalist notion of midrash (all is revealed on Sinai), 86–88; midrash at its maximum (God's nearness permits rabbinic freedom to interpret), 108–12; l'drosh (to seek, to interpret), 14, 54
Mipnei chatotenu galinu me'artsenu ("We were exiled from our land on account of our sins"), 18
Mishnah, xiii, xvi, xxii, xxvi, 4, 11, 28, 40, 41, 47–49, 58, 60, 62, 63, 68–71, 74–75, 77–78, 81–88, 94–97, 101, 110, 113
M'lokh al kol ha'olam b'khvodekha ("Rule over all the world in your full glory," from the Rosh Hashanah Amidah), x–xi, xvii, xix–xxi, 13, 17, 35–38, 45, 58, 105, 115
Moses, xxi, 54, 62, 67, 73–91, 96–97, 101, 105
myth-making, xxvii, 6, 11

Nebuchadnezzar, 21–22, 30, 40
Nitschuni banai, ("My children have overcome me,"), 109–10, 116

orthodoxy, xii–xviii, xx, xxviii, 3–4,7–8, 34–37, 68, 89–98

Pagam (maculation, fault, blemish), xi, xvii–xxi, 12–13, 47–8, 51, 53–4, 56–63, 68–71, 88–101, 106–16
piety (life of discsiplined religiosity), xiii–xxii, 8, 49–50
prayer, liturgy, x–xi, xiii, xvii, xx, xxii, xxv, xxvii, 3–7, 12–13, 15–17,

19–24, 28, 34–38, 41, 49, 58, 62, 68, 105–6, 107, 115–16; after Shoah, x–xi, xiii, xvii, xxvii, 12–13, 35, 40, 105–6, 115–16; Amidah, 17, 36; devotion (*devekut*), 12, 16; God's prayers, 44–46; in the Shoah, xxviii, 3–7, 15–17, 28, 34–38, 40, 68, 105, 107; *Kavanah* (intentionality), 15–17, 115–16; Machzor (for Rosh Hashanah), 3, 15, 40; *Modim*, prayer of thanksgiving, 109, 115; Rosh Hashanah, 3, 15–17, 28, 36, 90, 115; "Rule over all the world in your full glory" (*see M'lokh*); Sabbath, 28, 36–38, 81; holiday, 28, 36–38, 81, 87, 90; petition: 135–36, 41; Birkat hamazon ("Grace After Meals"), 41

Prosbul, 58, 63

R. Ashi, 62–63, 78, 81, 91
R. Elazar b. Azariah, 84, 101
R. Eliezer, 40, 85, 101, 110–13
R. Joshua, 110–12
R. Shimon b. Lakish, 3–18
R.Yehoshua b. Levi, 87–88, 101
R. Yishmael, 95
R. Yochanan (Amora), 34, 87
R. Yochanan b. Zakkai, 85
Rabbi Raba b. Nachman, 112
Rashbam (Rabbi Shmuel son of Meir, 11–12th cent.), xxii, xxix, 62
Ravina, 62–63
reasoning (logic, logical argument), xiv–xvi, xxvi, xxviii–xxix, 31, 45, 49, 60, 78, 80, 85, 106, 110, 113–14
Remnant of Judah (*sh'erit yehuda*), 21–22, 30, 40, 90–91
Revelation, x–xi, 11–13, 53–54, 73–100, 107–16

Romans, 29–30
Rosenzweig, Franz, xxviii–xxix
Roskies, David, 11–14

Sabbath, Shabbat, 28, 36–38, 41, 81, 90
Satan, 17, 20
Schiffman, Lawrence, 93–94, 101
Saboraim, 69
scholarship, textual, Talmudic: scientific (*see* science); religious historiography: xxi, xxv, 7, 10–14, 46–47, 105; plain sense historiography, xx, xxiii–xxv, 9, 13, 47–48, 105; deeper plain sense historiography: xxiv–xxv, 14, 48, 105; depth historiography: xxi–xxii, xxv–xxix, 7–10, 13–14, 46–49, 105
science, scientific judgment, xxii–xxviii, 13, 49–50, 105–106; science and piety, science and prayer, xix–xxviii, 11–13, 48–50, 67–71, 105–106, 107–16; Science of Judaism (das Wissenschaft des Judentums), xiv–xix; Textual and Historical science, 9–10, 13–14, 46–51, 67–71, 105–106
Sighet, xii, 4
sin, xvii–xviii, 3–4, 6, 9, 13–14, 17–40, 59, 62, 100; Golden Calf, 2–1, 2–8, 3–36, 4–9, 4–11, 59, 100; Sins of Israel (*chate'u yisrael*), xvii, xxv, xxvii, 8–10, 53–54, 68, 71
Sinai, x–xi, xviii–xxiv, xxvi, 11, 13, 53–54, 59, 62, 67–71, 73–100, 107–16
Spiritual Life, x, xix, xx, 6, 28–29, 36, 49, 58, 93, 107, 114
Stammaim, 69–71

suffering, v, xiii, xviii–xx, 3–6,
 10–13, 16–39, 59, 61, 98

Tannaim, *tannaitic*, xi, xvii, xxi, xxiii,
 29, 41, 55–60, 67–69, 81–86, 94,
 109–12
Temple: destruction of, 6, 11,
 21–22, 28–29, 54; In Memory of
 (*zekher l'mikdash*), 29; service: 22
theodicy, xxvi, 8–9
theology, xviii, xxi, xxiii, xxv, xxvi,
 3–8, 10–13, 16–17, 32, 40–41,
 46, 67–8, 76, 84–86, 96–101,
 1–6; Jewish, xiii–xiv, xviii–xxii,
 xxv–xxviii, 45–48, 67–69, 71,
 74–76, 96–101, 107–16;
 Holocaust (Jewish theology of),
 xiii, xxviii–xxix, 3–8, 10–13,
 16–17, 27, 32, 40–41, 45–48, 71,
 76, 96–15, 119
tikkun ("repair"), xiii, xviii, 7, 19, 24
 38, 48, 51, 55, 58–59, 63, 89;
 tikkun hamikra ("repairing
 Scripture"), xxviii, 53–63;
 restoring Scripture: xx–xxi, xxvii
 12 13 33 48–50, 53–63, 71, 75,
 96, 98–100, 108; *tikkun ha-olam*
 ("repairing the world—or the
 social order"), 55, 57–59, 63;
 writing as repairing, 8–13
Torah, Scripture: (*see also* Bible);
 Dual Torah, 73–100; forgotten
 (neglected): xvii, xxv–xxvii,
 53–58, 68, 89–92; interpretation
 of, to interpret ("l'drosh") (*see*
 Midrash); literal meaning of,
 xxiii–xxiv, 12, 23, 24, 60–62, 70,
 84, 87, 91, 108, 110–16;
 maculation of (*see Pagam*); Oral
 (*she b'al peh*), xi, xix, xxi, 53–54,
 67–71, 73–100, 108–16; plain
 sense of (*peshat*), xi, xiv,
 xvii–xxviii, 8–13, 45–50, 68–71,
 86, 105–10, 114; Written (*she
 b'khtav*), xxi, 17–23, 53–54,
 57–62, 68, 73–100, 108–16;
 Restored (*see Tikkun*); study of
 (*talmud torah*), x–xi, xiv–xxix,
 4–13, 28–29, 45, 48–50, 53, 59,
 87, 94, 97, 105, 107, 115; *Torat
 emet* ("the plain truths of
 Torah"), 48, 59, 69; Unwritten
 (unwritten law), 73, 83, 90–93;
 tikkun hamikra or "repairing
 Scripture" (*see Tikkun*)
Tosafists, Tosafot, 41, 63, 88, 111
Truth, xv–xix, xxiv, 36, 48, 60, 68,
 99

Wissenschaft des judentums,
 xiv–xvi. *See also* scholarship
Wolfsberg Labor Camp. *See*
 concentration camps

Yad Vashem, xxviii, 3, 15, 40
Yeshivah, xiv, xx, xxviii, 38, 39; *roshe*
 (heads of religous academy), 8,
 47, 71

About the Author

David Weiss Halivni is Professor Emeritus of Classical Jewish Civilization at Columbia University. Halivni survived the concentration camps of Auschwitz, Wolfsberg, and Mathausen—where his entire family was put to death. Most widely known for his scholarly commentary on the Talmud, *Mekorot Umasorot* ("Sources and Traditions"), Halivni has also written a series of more general studies of classic rabbinic literature, the most recent of which was *Revelation Restored: Divine Writ and Critical Responses*. He has also published his memoirs, *The Book and the Sword: A Life of Learning in the Shadow of Destruction*. Prior to his appointment at Columbia University, he was for thirty years professor of Rabbinics at the Jewish Theological Seminary of New York. He now resides in Jerusalem, where he offers lectures at the Hebrew University and Bar-Ilan University.

About the Editor

Peter Ochs is Edgar Bronfman Professor of Modern Judaic Studies at the University of Virginia. He is co-founder of the Society for Scriptural Reasoning, and The Society for Textual Reasoning. Among his books are *Another Reformation: Postliberal Christianity and the Jews; Peirce, Pragmatism and the Logic of Scripture; Reviewing the Covenant* (with Eugene Borowitz); and *Reasoning after Revelation: Dialogues in Postmodern Jewish Philosophy* (coauthored).